A PHYSICIAN'S
DIARY

A PHYSICIAN'S DIARY

Case Histories of Hope and Healing
with Edgar Cayce's
and Other Natural Remedies

by Dr. Dana Myatt

A.R.E. Press • Virginia Beach • Virginia

A.R.E. Press
Sixty-Eighth & Atlantic Avenue
P.O. Box 656
Virginia Beach, VA 23451-0656

AUTHOR'S NOTE:

The stories contained herein are meant to inspire and educate the reader. No part of this book is intended to substitute for competent medical diagnosis.

Each of the cases portrayed in this book involve patients who received treatments that were specific for them and their condition.

Readers are cautioned and encouraged to seek the advice of a competent medical practitioner who can advise how best to apply concepts and therapies discussed in this book for your specific condition.

Biblical quotes are from a parallel Bible published by Reader's Digest and include the following versions: King James, the Living Bible, Revised Standard, and the New International.

Library of Congress Cataloging-in-Publication Data

Myatt, Dana, 1959-

A physician's diary: case histories of hope and healing from Edgar Cayce's and other natural remedies / by Dana Myatt.

    p. cm.

ISBN 87604-316-3

1. Myatt, Dana, 1959- . 2. Naturopaths—United States—Biography. I. Title.

RZ439.7.M9583 1994

610'.92-dc20   93-48912

Cover design by Patti McCambridge

TABLE OF CONTENTS

FOREWORD

Edgar Cayce said, "There are in truth no incurable conditions . . . healing depends upon the individual . . . " (3744-2)

Jesus the Christ, when asked if it were possible to cure a particular disease, responded, "All things are possible to those who believe." (Mark 9:23)

An old proverb, its origin obscure to me, says, "Where there's life, there's hope."

My personal scientific understanding, as well as my clinical observation, have led me to conclude that the foregoing statements are true. I have personally witnessed cures that were not thought to be possible. I will be sharing some of these "impossible cures" with you in the pages that follow.

Many times individuals come to me after they have exhausted conventional medical methods of diagnosis and treatment. "You are my last hope," they tell me. The problem is that by the time I am "the last hope," that individual has nearly *lost* hope. The longer someone has struggled with an illness and the more treatments that have been tried and have failed, the stronger the feeling of hopelessness can be.

The comfort to me is that, if I am a "last hope," a flicker of hope still remains. If that flicker can be fanned into a flame, the possibility of cure increases. This book is intended to fan the flames of hope for those who are physically or emotionally afflicted and for those who wish to help heal themselves should they become stricken. There is no such thing as "false hope." Hope is always genuine and cure is always possible.

The case histories in this book are real. They represent just a few of the miracles of hope and healing that I have been fortunate to witness and to participate in. If you have found yourself with a difficult illness, take heart! There are others who have had similar difficulties and have emerged victorious. You can, too.

I am confident that you will also recognize that many valuable healing methods are available to you. Some are found in conventional Western medicine and some are not. The cures described in this book came about as the results of a full *complement* of healing methods. It is often the willingness to consider *all* the healing choices that gives us the surest and swiftest results.

My hope is that this book will entertain, enlighten, or inspire you. Who knows? Perhaps it will do all three.

In health,
Dana Myatt, N.D.

ACKNOWLEDGMENTS

This book came to me through *my* head and hand, but it is really the work of many people. I would like to thank some of them now . . .

Flo and Ray Wishmeyer, alias "Mom and Dad," who did a sterling job of raising me in spite of the challenges I presented to them.

Maxine Meyer, my dear friend and mentor, without whose help this book would still be just an idea. She countered my every excuse with a creative idea or a nag (whichever was most appropriate at the time), and she didn't let up until the work was completed. Everyone should be so lucky to have such a friend.

Joe Dunn, my tireless editor-in-chief, who continues to be encouraging and supportive.

Dr. Jack Daugherty, my naturopathic medical mentor.

And most important, every patient who ever entered my life.

You are all my valued teachers and friends.

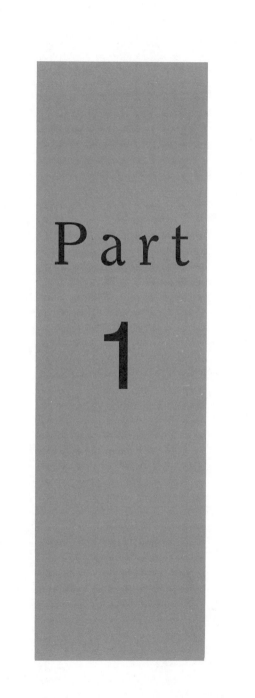

Part

1

1

THE DECISION

The man towering over me looked like a ghostly shadow against the glaring overhead lights of the emergency room. Pain shot through my body as he vigorously scrubbed my scalded belly with a brush. "Oh, *please* stop," I cried. "*Please* don't use that brush."

"Be quiet," he scolded gruffly. "This doesn't hurt."

Oh, but it *did* hurt. It hurt more than anything I had ever felt.

Some have said that when people face death, their lives flash before their eyes. At only eight years old, one might think that the flash of remembrance would go quickly. Somehow, the intense pain caused me to reflect back on childhood memories in slow motion. Recalling my life's story seemed to take me away from the intense pain of the moment.

I had heard my mother tell the story of my birth so many times that I felt as if I actually remembered it. My only brother was eighteen years old when my mother became pregnant with me. As Mom tells it, she really didn't think that she was pregnant. Perhaps it was the "change of life." After several months with a growing abdomen and waves of nausea, she knew. Not having considered the possibility of another child, she was taken by surprise. Fortunately for me, the thought of having a baby girl thrilled her. She was certain, she said, that I would be a girl. When friends would ask her, "What do you want?" she would say, "A girl." Then they would scold, "Now, Flo, what you *really* want is just a healthy baby, right?" "No," she'd say, "I want a girl, and I *know* this baby is a girl."

Several months before I was born, my mother left the man who was my genetic father. A physically abusive man, he had beaten her badly on many occasions. At seven months' pregnant she sustained physical injuries that made her fear for both our lives. Wanting us *both* to be safe, she left. I, the baby inside her belly, became even more precious to her. With my brother ready to leave home, Mom and I would be each others' family.

My mother expected me to be born on Saint Patrick's Day, and she was going to name me Kelly. The date came and went. Alas, my mother contemplated a different name. Two days after my expected arrival, the labor pains began. Mother went to the nearest hospital, a Catholic hospital, to give birth to me.

The labor and delivery went smoothly. As soon as I was delivered, however, the doctors discovered that something was wrong. I wasn't breathing. They whisked me away to another room, and soon after that the nuns came in and offered to say the last rites on my behalf. They told my mother that I would not live, that my lungs were filled with fluid. None of the doctors in the hospital were experienced with this particular problem. It was not a common occurrence. "No," my mother told them sternly. It was more of a refusal to God than to the nuns. "Please just go away. Leave me alone." They left, my mother told me, and *she* had a very serious conversation with God.

Like many people in this country, my mother attended church regularly. She believed in a Supreme Being, but she was not particularly religious. At this moment, however, she was desperate. I know her prayer came from the very depths of her soul. She called out to the Supreme Being in whatever way that she understood Him/Her to be and made a bargain. "Let my baby girl live," she pleaded, "and I promise to raise her as a good Christian girl." It seems fitting that my birthplace was Sacramento, California, for the name means "sacrament," and the root word in Latin, *sacer*, means "holy" or "consecrated to God."

Somehow, after her pleading prayer, she said that she felt a peace, a *certainty* that she had been heard. She *knew* I would live. Exhausted from childbirth but previously unable to sleep, she now relaxed into a peaceful state.

Elsewhere in the hospital a visiting doctor was making rounds. He was in town for one day to teach at a local university and was touring the hospital as part of his visit. A specialist in newborn resuscitation, he happened to be present in the neonatal intensive care unit when I was brought in. Patrick Kennedy, the third child born to John and Jackie Kennedy, suffered from the same condition, and this was the doctor who had attempted to resuscitate him. Our "coincidental" meeting saved my life. Patrick had not been so fortunate.

Two hours later, after my birth, predicted death, and rebirth, the nuns tied my thick black hair with a tiny pink bow and brought me to my mother. Her prayers had been answered. I was alive. And Mother had made a promise to the Almighty that she was bound and determined to keep.

For the first four years of my life it was just my mom and me. My older brother had gone to join the Coast Guard and my mother reared me. By day she worked as a beautician in a small town beauty salon. Though we never had much money, my mother always gave me the very best she could afford. Instead of buying herself a new pair of shoes, I got a bright new stroller and a gingham dress with ruffles. Grandma and Grandpa baby-sat me in the daytime. Being the only baby girl in the family, I was treasured by my relatives. Grandma and I would work in the garden and go for picnics in the park behind her house. Grandpa and I would play games we invented, and I would entertain him with my singing from the fireplace hearth.

My conscious recollection of my life really began one evening when I was four years old. Momma had dressed me in some of my finest things, including my black patent leather shoes and white ankle socks with ruffles around the top. She was dressed up like she did for church, but it wasn't Sunday. I remember her washing dishes and telling me that pretty soon a man would be coming to the door. "He is a nice man," she told me. "Someone that my friend arranged for me to meet." Momma and the man were going square-dancing together and I would go to Grandma's. I was told to sit at the front window and watch for the man to come.

A gold station wagon stopped in front of the house. It was so clean that it sparkled in the setting rays of the sun. Out of the car stepped The Man—tall, regal, and handsome. He looked to me like a knight stepping out of a shining carriage. I watched in fascination as he came to the front door. "Momma, he's here! He's here!" I hollered, and I ran to the front door before she could dry her hands. I opened the door myself and there he stood. Though my momma had taught me to be wary of strangers, somehow this man was not a stranger to me. I threw my arms wide in the gesture of a hug and he picked me up off the ground and hugged me back. I felt as if I had known him my whole life, just as I always knew Momma.

Several months later, my mother told me that she and The Man would be getting married. "I saw him first! I saw him first!" I reminded her. "Yes, and you'll get to have him, too," she told me. "He's going to be your daddy." I was so excited I could hardly breathe. This man was very nice to Momma. He was very nice to me, too, and now it would be the three of us! The news of their engagement was the first time I recall feeling joyful. Now I knew what it meant to be "bursting with joy."

Momma and The Man, whose name was Ray Wishmeyer, were married. Shortly after they returned from a vacation (Grandma said it was a honeymoon), I was dressed and ready to go to the courthouse. Momma said this was the day when we would sign papers that would officially make Ray my dad. I remember standing before a big bench and a man with a black robe. He said some words to both of them and then he spoke to me. He told me that I now had a father, and for a second time I felt as if I would burst from joy.

Now I had both a mom and a dad, and we moved to a big house that had dogs and horses. The house that we lived in, in my small eyes, was magnificent. It was out in the country and surrounded by acres of trees. It was the most beautiful thing I could imagine. The living room overlooked a huge deck which overlooked a mountainside. Windows went all the way to the ceiling, and the ceiling was very high. There were three huge stone fireplaces. How wonderful it was to sit in front of the fire when it was snowing outside! My father had built the house himself after he retired from the navy. With plans and drawings collected and refined over his many years in the service, the house had taken him seven years to build. From those huge fireplaces to the mag-

nificently crafted oak cabinets to the redwood deck, he had
built it all himself. It was a wonderful place to live and it was
filled with love.

We had been in the house less than a year at Christmas
time. Mom, Dad, and I left our country abode and went to
the city to do Christmas shopping. By the time we came
home, it was night. Driving deeper into the forest, the area
where we lived, we saw a bright orange glow above the trees.
As we got closer, it became clear that it was caused by a fire.
It looked like it was in the direction of our house, and I remember Mother saying, "Oh no! I hope it's not Andy's place.
Poor Andy." As we got closer we saw with horror that it was
not Andy's place—it was *our* place. Fire trucks, with lights
flashing, filled the yard. Neighbors were standing with their
garden hoses in their hands. The entire house was ablaze.
Flames leaped so high that the surrounding pine trees were
catching fire. The small trickles from the neighbors' garden
hoses seemed laughable compared to the size of the fire.
While Mom and I stood and watched in horror, my father
went over and spoke to one of the firemen. We saw him
pointing in two directions and then he came back to us. He
told us that the firemen didn't know where the irrigation
ditches were. After their trucks were empty, they had been
out of water. Alas, the neighbors with their garden hoses
were there to help.

The three of us—my mom, my dad, and I—stood and
watched as our beautiful house went up in flames. My
mother and I were sobbing. Seven long years of my dad's
loving efforts were going up in flames. Furniture, memen-
tos, and specialties collected from around the world while
he was in the navy were gone in a few short hours. Even at
my young age, I understood what the fire meant. I understood the shock, the grief, the loss, as we watched our house
burn like a giant bonfire in the night. My father stood mo-
tionless and mute. "How could he not be crying like mother

and I?" I wondered to myself. Then he spoke, and my mother and I both knew how much we loved this man. "Thank God," he said with a trembling voice, "that none of my family was in that house."

The days that followed just after were a blur. A collection was taken up at church for clothes and household items. We had lost everything in the fire except for the clothes on our backs and each other. Someone gave us a small travel trailer to live in, and I remember the three of us being parked in Grandma and Grandpa's driveway. Though he never complained, Dad was in some degree of shock. We had to go and inspect the ruins of our house for insurance purposes. The three majestic stone fireplaces were left standing. Globs of melted silver were the only indication of where the dining room had been. A set of Corning Ware® bowls, undamaged by the fire, marked the kitchen. One of the fireman had made a valiant rescue effort by running into the bedroom and grabbing items to be saved. The only thing he had managed to bring out safely was a box. That box contained all of the family photograph albums. We were grateful to have those family memories left intact.

Another young firefighter standing on the deck was severely burned when a portion of the house exploded. The shattered glass and force of the flame had blown him off the deck. Badly fractured, cut, and severely burned, he lay in intensive care at the local hospital for days. I remember my mother and grandmother going to visit him every day.

The house and property had been insured for less than half its value. Even with sufficient funds, I don't think my dad would have gone back and rebuilt that house. Though I know he was genuinely thankful that the items of true importance were saved, it was still painful to see the burned wreckage.

As soon as we were able, we bought a new house—a big duplex on a large piece of property. My father went to work building another structure, a beauty salon for my mother. It would be the biggest and most elegant salon in town. Their plans for the salon were spoken of day and night. It would be a lovely place where the patrons would be made to feel like royalty. It would cost patrons no more to come here than to go any place else, but the quality would be the best available. They would name it "The Red Carpet."

So, our new life was every bit as grand, though different, from the old. My mother was owner and manager of a lovely beauty salon. My father worked days as an engineer and at night did the bookkeeping for the beauty shop. I enjoyed spending time alone in my free-standing tree house, which we called a ranger station, and climbing apple and walnut trees in the small orchard.

Finally, at age five, it was time for me to start school. I already knew the alphabet because my dad had taught it to me one day on a trip to the dump. Whenever Dad needed to haul a load of leaves to the local garbage dump, he would ask me to ride with him. It was "our time" together because Mom usually wasn't inclined to go. Ordinarily, we'd sing to-gether—off key and loud. One day, instead of our usual songfest, he offered to teach me the alphabet. "If we work real hard," he told me, "you can learn the whole alphabet by the time we get home. You can surprise your mother with it. When you can say it all the way through without any mis-takes, I'll buy you a stuffed animal." The thought of surprising my mom and the offer of a new stuffed pet were irresistible. And so, in that hour it took to go to the dump, I learned to say the alphabet. I was rewarded by a hug from my mother and a bright red-and-yellow stuffed billy goat from my father.

In kindergarten and first grade, I went to public schools. My mother came to pick me up early one day for a dentist appointment. When she found me eating my lunch outside in the rain, she was angry. "Why are you sitting in the rain eating your lunch?" she demanded to know.

"Because the teacher won't let us eat indoors. We always have to eat lunch outside. It's the rule," I informed her. After that, my parents put me in a Catholic school.

True to my mother's word, I was raised as a "good Christian girl." Mother, father, and I attended the Episcopal church and Sunday school nearly every week. Like most kids, I thought Sunday school was O.K. and church was not. I liked the singing and Father was a jolly man, but sitting still for church was difficult. Catholic school didn't seem very different from church. The priest wore the same kind of black clothes with a white collar as Father Don did at our church. Nuns with black dresses and black hair coverings were new to me, but I quickly settled in and it didn't seem so strange. I liked Catholic school. When the teachers discovered that I could read bigger words than those in my reader, they put me in a special reading class. There, we got to read *real* stories about real people. With Dick, Jane, Sally, and their dog Spot off my required reading list and out of my life, I was pretty happy.

There was something extra in Catholic school that we didn't have in public school. It was a class called Catechism. In this class, Father O'Connor, a young, tall, and handsome priest, would come in and talk to us about God. Father O'Connor at Catholic school dressed the same as Father Don at Episcopal church. Sister Danielle, our homeroom teacher, was young and beautiful and sweet. It seemed to me that she and Father O'Connor would make a perfect couple. Why hadn't someone thought of this before? I just couldn't understand. In the Episcopal church, priests get married. One day during Catechism when Father O'Connor asked if there were any questions, I raised my hand boldly and shook it around to get his attention. "Father, I have a question," I stated, to emphasize its importance. "Why don't you and Sister Danielle get married?" Instead of the praise for my brilliant idea that I expected, I was met by uproarious laughter from my classmates. Father O'Connor was speechless and Sister Danielle turned a bright shade of red. I didn't know what I had done, but I felt ashamed. I opened the lid to my desk drawer, pretending to look for a pencil in a feeble effort to hide. When I closed the lid, I accidentally shut it on my hand. My question, so lovingly and deliberately conceived, had turned to shambles. I was humiliated emotionally and now hurt physically. Later that day, Sister Danielle took me aside and explained to me that nuns and priests are not allowed to marry. I wanted to argue, to tell her that priests *could* marry. I knew this for a fact because Father Don at our church was married. Instead, I remained silent.

Several weeks later, Father O'Connor came to teach us about God. Catechism class was better than mathematics, I decided. I already sort of understood who God was from church. God was like the King of the Universe. Father O'Connor said that God was the Supreme Being, Master, Maker, Ruler of everything. That sounded reasonable to me. Then he began to describe the nature of God. He said that God was all powerful. This meant that all of the power that existed belonged to God. Any power that a person had was given to him or her by God because all of the power belonged to God. This sounded reasonable to me, too. Like one of the characteristics you would expect from a God, a Supreme Being.

Then Father said that God was omnipresent. This meant, he said, that God was every place—in the world, in the sky, in the universe, and beyond the universe. He said that there was no place that God was not. This, too, sounded reasonable to me, considering that God was King of the Universe.

Finally, and most important, according to Father, God was *all loving*, and he read to us from the Bible where it said, "God is love." He told us that there was nothing about God's nature that was contrary to love. I just *knew* that this was correct. A Supreme Being in charge of everything must *certainly* be all loving. I believed that. Then Father told us about hell. He said that hell was a very hot place, and if we didn't do things right we would go to that very hot place for eternity. I knew that eternity meant "the rest of forever." Now I had another question.

I was a little shy to ask another question, of course. It had only been two weeks earlier that I had humiliated myself by asking a stupid question. Maybe if I kept silent and waited a little longer, my question would be answered without my asking. But the thought of spending forever in a really hot place frightened me and so I had to ask. In spite of my hesitation, I raised my hand slowly and waited to be called on. When Father gave me the nod, I cleared my throat and proceeded cautiously. "Father," I asked, "if God is all powerful, and if God is every place that is, and if God is all loving, where is hell and why would He send us there?" The room was silent; Father was silent. He stared at me and I stared back at him for what seemed like a very long time. I could tell from the look on his face that I had just asked an important question. In fact, the longer we stared at each other, the more I began to realize that I had just asked an adult a question for which the adult had no answer.

At the end of the long silence, Father cleared his throat and said, "Leap of faith." Then he went on to say some other things that didn't really make sense to me. When he finished, in my mind, the question was left unanswered.

In the third grade I became fascinated with science. At every chance I would go the library and look at biology books. Because my reading ability was ahead of my grade level, I could read the books of the eighth-grade science classes. The human body particularly fascinated me. When I found a book about conception and the development of the baby inside the mother's womb, I checked it out of the library and carried it with me for over a month.

I wasn't sure that I understood enough about this God-fellow. I knew people talked about Him in church and in school. And I knew when I began studying science that there was some sort of a Creator. The design of nature, the patterns, the complexity, *surely* did not happen by accident. Though I didn't know who or what God was, I believed there was some sort of a Supreme Intelligence. It seemed intuitively obvious to me from all these wonders of nature.

At eight years old I was mature for my age. My parents knew if they gave me a task to do, I could do it. Finally, one great day came when my mother trusted me to be at home alone with a playmate. She was going golfing for the morning and was going to get a sitter for me and my friend. I convinced her that I could be trusted to stay home alone. After all, the beauty shop with lots of grown-ups was only a few steps away from the house. Grandma was only a phone call away. And my friend Theresa and I would be playing in the orchard, and there would be somebody close by if we needed help. I promised to be good. Considering how responsible I had always been and the apparent safety of the situation, my mother trusted me without a baby-sitter this morning. Everything was already prepared for lunch; tuna salad was in the refrigerator. I was going to surprise my girl friend by making us tuna sandwiches.

When lunch time came, I had a bold idea. Tuna sandwiches were O.K. but Mexican food would be better. I had seen my mother cook tacos before, and I knew I could do it. It didn't seem risky—just a little deviation from the plan. And so I took the tortillas out of the freezer and heated hot oil on the stove. I put the tortillas in the pan. The hot grease spattered and popped, but that was O.K. That's how Mom did it. With spatula in hand, I climbed on a chair and scraped hard to loosen the snapping tortillas. As I did, I pulled the pan of hot oil onto my belly. The pain was excruciating, but I didn't move. My little friend, Theresa, began screaming and hollering hysterically. "Calm down," I told her, "it's O.K." I went to the sink and got a glass of cold water and poured it on myself. I could already see the big blisters rising on my abdomen. My gingham dress was melted onto my flesh. Trying futilely to calm my friend, I called one of the operators in the shop. "Please come next door to the house. I have poured some hot oil on myself." Next I called Grandma. "Grandma," I said, "I did a bad thing. Mom is going to kill me. I burned myself."

"I will be right there," Grandma said. I had only two thoughts in my mind: calm my girlfriend who was hysterical, and how would I explain this to my mom. By now I wasn't feeling any pain from the burn. I didn't know how long it took, but Grandma arrived at the house and loaded me in a taxi cab and we drove together to the hospital. All the way there I remembered thinking that I had let my mother down. I kept repeating over and over to Grandma, "Mother will kill me. Mother will kill me." I wasn't really worried that mother would hurt me. I was worried that I had broken her trust. When I arrived at the emergency room, the doctor peeled my dress off my burned abdomen. Some of the blisters were over an inch high. I felt no physical pain, only the emotional pain of having broken my mother's trust. No pain, that is, until this man started scrubbing my belly with a brush.

Suddenly, I was back to the bright lights and the excruciating sensation of brush on raw flesh. "Please! Please stop!" I begged. "Be quiet! This doesn't hurt," the voice commanded. How dare he say that, I thought to myself. How does he know it doesn't hurt? It *does* hurt. It hurts more than anything I have ever known. And in that moment I *knew*— I had made my decision: when I grow up, I am going to be a doctor. I'm going to do what this man does, only better. Because when I'm a doctor, I'm going to be kind.

2

MEETING EDGAR CAYCE

I recovered quickly from the "burned belly incident." My mother never scolded me. My remorse at having broken her trust must have been apparent to her—for she never said a word about the incident. Her only expression was one of concern for my recovery.

It was fortunate, I realized even then, that I had had the experience. After all, it was that emergency room doctor who helped me see what I wanted to be when I grew up. I wasn't sure if I could actually be a doctor, however. When I went to the doctor, the doctor was always a male. Females were always nurses. Still, I had it in my mind that I wanted to be a doctor.

Several weeks after making my decision, I went to my

mother. "Mom," I announced tentatively, "I want to be a doctor when I grow up. Is that O.K.?"

"What kind of a doctor do you mean?" she asked. I was surprised at the question.

"You know," I told her, "the kind of doctor who helps people get healthy. The kind of doctor that takes care of you when you are sick."

"Oh," she said with full recognition. "Of course, that's O.K. You can do whatever you want to do, but go double-check with your father."

"Dad," I announced, now with more confidence, "I've decided that I want to be a doctor when I grow up. Is that O.K.?"

"Why sure, honey," he affirmed. "You can be whatever you want to be. You just have to be sure you do something you really like doing so that you'll be good at it. If you're going to be a doctor," he counseled, "you'd better start saving your money now. It costs a lot of money to go to medical school." Even at my tender age, his words seemed reasonable. "Here's what I'll do," he continued. "For every bit of money that you save toward medical school, I'll match it with a similar amount of money."

Though I thought I understood what he meant, I pressed for clarification. "Does that mean if I save money from my allowance, you'll put the same amount of money with it and we'll save it together?" I wanted to know.

"Yes," he confirmed. "If you save fifty cents from your allowance, I'll put another fifty cents with it, and together we'll save a dollar for your medical school tuition fund."

Though I have never considered mathematics to be my forte, this seemed like a good financial move to me. From age eight on, I began to save for what was known as my "medical school tuition fund." Every week I would put aside fifty cents of my one dollar allowance for this fund. If I knew then just how expensive medical school would be, I might have saved seventy-five cents or the whole dollar!

Now my direction was clear to me. I was going to be a doctor when I grew up. Adults seemed often inclined to ask me, "What will you be when you grow up?" My reply was confident and certain. "I'm going to be a doctor," I would announce, and they would chuckle. I always wondered why they chuckled. Then they spoke and I knew.

"Oh, that's good," they'd tell me. "But you'll probably change your mind many times before you're big."

"No, I won't," I told them. "I'm certain." Then they'd laugh again and I'd laugh, too. They were laughing at me with my childlike certainty. I was laughing at them, for their adult-like certainty.

Also from that age, I began reading— studying everything I could about science. I would go to the library and check out books that told about life, biology, creation. One book I found called *A Child Is Born* was my favorite for many months. Its pictures documented conception and birth of a baby. I was fascinated, and I carried the book with me wherever I went. I read it so often the pages were tattered, but I had memorized them all.

In my mind, a picture was forming. I was starting to know what kind of a doctor I wanted to be. I knew I wanted to be kind—kinder than the man who had treated me in the emergency room. I wanted to be smart, to know as much as I could about science and the body. That was all I knew, but I clung to it.

I also told my granny about my plans. My mother's mother was the only grandmother I had ever known. Granny, as I always called her, was my "most special person." There was something about Granny, *my* Granny, that was different from anyone else I knew. She always seemed to understand everything; she always seemed to accept everything. When I told her that I was going to be a doctor, she nodded and said, "I'm so glad. You'll be a good one." To me, that made it certain. You see, Granny always had "the gift."

We never talked about it much in our family; we just always knew. Granny was different. Granny had "the gift."

My grandmother June, or "Junie" as we called her, was different from other grandmothers. Granny never seemed old. She was timeless. Everyone—family and friends—knew they could go to Junie and have a listening ear. She was never one to gossip. Secrets were always safe with Granny. She was never one to judge or criticize. It seemed you could tell her anything and she would listen and understand. She didn't let people get away with being lazy, judgmental, or proud, however. Somehow, in her own inimitable way, she would gently counsel us back to reasonability. No matter what the problem, no matter what we felt our personality defect was, we could talk to Granny. Her advice was always sound.

There was something else about Granny. Granny had this ability "to know." Never religious, she entered church only at Christmas and Easter time, and only at the pleadings of the family. Still, she seemed to know God better than anybody I knew. In addition to her wisdom and her spirit, which seemed to attract everyone, Granny always *knew.* If Granny warned to be careful of this or that, everyone in the family had come to take it seriously. A warning from Granny was as good as gold. She *knew.* Somehow she could foresee events with uncanny accuracy. At family gatherings, we would always ask Granny to tell our fortunes with the cards. Though she had learned to tell fortunes in the "regular way" (whatever that is), we knew she did something else. She would "see" things and report those in the fortune. Granny was special. Granny always *knew.*

She never spoke of her gift. In fact, I think it annoyed her greatly. She didn't ask for it, didn't want it. One time when I asked her why, she told me: "More often," she said, "it's the bad things I see. If someone's in danger or in trouble, that comes to me. Not so often the good things, but more often the bad things."

"Don't you see, Granny," I told her, "you know those things so you can warn us."

"Yes," she said, "I suppose it's a gift. But I never did ask for it. And it's rather a nuisance."

I remember one day being downtown with Granny and my Great Auntie Marge. Granny's sister always liked to brag about Granny's gift. Somehow a conversation came up in a store. Auntie Marge announced loudly, "My sister's psychic" and nodded at Granny. Granny was not one to blush, but on this day I could see her face red hot.

A man that none of us knew sauntered up cockily. "Oh yeah," he said, as he stared my grandmother in the face. "If you're so psychic, tell me something about myself."

Without hesitation, Granny looked at his eyes and said, "You served time on the Georgia chain gang."

The man's face was aghast. "So help me, lady," he hollered, shaking his fist in her face, "if you ever tell any-body, I'll kill you." After the long silence that followed, he said, "You know me."

"Do you know me?" Granny asked simply and without fear.

"No," the man replied.

"Well," said Granny, "I don't know you either. I've never seen you." The man blinked and then walked quickly away.

Mother went swimming one time. She dove into a pool that was shallower than she had thought. Hitting the bottom of the pool, she scraped all of the skin off her chest and abdomen. Several days later, we were at Grandma's house. My mother's wounds were not visible with her clothes on.

"Oh, Flossie," my grandmother warned, as if suddenly remembering. "Please be careful, honey, when you go swimming. I'm very afraid that something will happen."

Mom and I looked at each other. "Don't worry, Mom," my own mother said. "It's already passed." She opened her shirt to reveal her wounds.

Yes, my granny had "the gift." She *knew.* Not that she wanted it; not that she looked for it. In fact, she would've been glad to give the gift away. In her later years, the gift seemed to subside, much to her apparent relief. My early experience with Granny taught me that some people have this gift. I didn't know anyone else but Granny who had it, but still I knew that some did.

From that frame of reference I met Edgar Cayce.

I was still planning to be a doctor at age twelve. It was then that I awoke in the middle of the night with severe abdominal pain. My temperature was high. I was nauseous and vomiting. The pain in my belly was severe. I called out in the night to my mother. Coming to my bedside she announced, "It might be appendicitis. We must take you to the emergency room." My experience with the earlier emergency room doctor flashed through my mind. "No, anything but that. Can't you try something else first?" I pleaded. I could see the fear in my mother's eyes. She went to her room, and I saw her reach underneath the bed and pull out a book. It was a black book and there were no markings on its cover. She brought it back into my bedroom and sat by my bedside as she thumbed through the pages. "Castor oil packs," she read aloud to me. The pain was too great, I was not listening. She left the room, prepared what I later found out was a castor oil pack, heated it in our microwave oven, and returned. She placed it over my ailing belly and the next thing I knew it was morning. The pack had taken away my pain and I was fine.

My natural instinct was one of curiosity. "Mother," I asked her, "what was that book you were reading from last night? What was that pack you put on me? It made my pain go away." That was my first true research mission as a future physician, though I might not have recognized it as such!

"Oh," my mother hedged, "it was 'the black book.' " She

was silent, hoping perhaps that my questioning would cease.

" 'The black book?' " I inquired. "What's a black book and why do you keep it under your bed?" I demanded to know.

"Well, honey," she started to explain . . .

"A man named Edgar Cayce," she told me, "had a gift of 'knowing.' Sort of like Granny. A lot of the information that he gave had to do with people and their health and illness and how to get them better."

"And the book that you read from?" I wanted to know.

"It's called 'the black book,' " she told me. "It has some of the readings from Edgar Cayce."

"What was a 'reading'?" I pressed her. "And why is the book kept under your bed?"

"Well," she said, "I'll give you a book to read and then you'll know about Edgar Cayce. The book will explain what the 'readings' are. I keep the book under the bed because, well . . . because not everybody would understand," she explained hesitantly. "Some people, like the people who go to our church, think that 'knowing' is evil."

"You mean like Granny's 'knowing?' " I was aghast.

"Yes, like Granny's 'knowing,' " she affirmed.

"But Granny's not evil," I pleaded as if trying to convince her. "Granny's the best person I know."

"Yes," she agreed. "I know that and you know that, but not everybody believes that. This way of 'knowing' like Granny does, well, some people think it's evil. Edgar Cayce, the man in 'the black book,' had a similar way of 'knowing.' Not everybody that we go to church with would understand."

I was still somewhat confused. "But, Mother," I argued with her, "Jesus knew."

She stared at me blankly. "What do you mean?"

"Well," I continued, "there were lots of times when Jesus just knew, like Granny, without anybody saying anything.

When the lady touched the hem of His robe and was healed—He knew that He had been touched. Even though He was in a crowd with lots of people who were touching Him, He knew that she wanted to be healed. And the night before He was crucified, He knew that someone would betray Him and He knew who it was. The people in our church don't believe *that* was evil," I said as if trying to convince her.

"Well, honey," my mother continued, "not everybody is as reasonable as you are. Not everybody knows Scripture as well as you do either," she said with a slight chuckle. "Yes, Jesus seemed to 'know.' For some reason there's a lot of people in our church who think it's evil if anybody else 'knows.' " I recognized her words to be true from what they had taught me in Sunday school, but I was still confused.

I continued, as if trying to convince her, "Don't you remember what Jesus said? 'Be ye perfect even as I am perfect.' Jesus said that His gift of knowing was that—a gift. And He told us to be like Him. Why would it be evil to have a gift like Jesus had?" My questions were becoming demanding.

"I don't know, honey. I just don't know why some people think that," my mother said frustratedly. "Here's 'the black book,' if you want to read it." She handed over the treasured document.

I read "the black book" from cover to cover. It was fascinating. Much information was given about physical health and healing. I could not tell from where it came—there was no description in the book. Some of the book talked about other things, like angels and life beyond this life. When I had finished the book, I returned to my mother for more information. "I still don't understand," I announced to her. "Where did this information come from? And I don't know who Edgar Cayce was." At that point, she gave me a book called *There Is a River* by Thomas Sugrue. This book told the life story of Edgar Cayce. Though I was fascinated by his story, it did not seem so peculiar. After all, Edgar Cayce was just a man who had "the gift." The gift—like Jesus had displayed, like Granny had. What was so unusual or so wrong with that?

From the book about his life, I began to read about Edgar Cayce. He was born outside of Hopkinsville, Kentucky, on March 18, 1877. His family was one of simple means, and he was always raised as a "good Christian boy." As the story unfolded, I read about the young Edgar Cayce. One thing that Edgar had always asked for above all other things was that he might be helpful to humankind. When he was ten, he was given a Bible, which he proceeded to read once through for every year of his life. At age thirteen, while enjoying time alone at his own "special spot," a female form appeared to him and asked him what he would like. Surprised by the vision, Edgar said that he would like to be helpful, especially to little children. The female figure left. Shortly thereafter Edgar was having a great deal of difficulty with his spelling lessons. His father, a stern man, was quizzing him on the spelling words. Edgar, it seemed, could spell nothing correctly. Finally, he heard a voice which told him that if he could sleep for just a few moments, "they" could help him. He begged his father for a brief nap. Dozing for ten minutes on his textbook, he awoke and knew the entire contents of the book. After that, Edgar was greatly assisted through school by sleeping on his textbooks.

During his formative years, there were other things that were "unusual" about him, but not so remarkable that anyone took great note. In addition to his peculiar way of learning, Edgar sometimes saw and played with children that no one else, except his mother, could see. Also, at a very tender age, he had a deep regard and fascination for the Bible. Still, in many ways he was like other youngsters. His curiosity about life and some of his early psychic gifts were not really appreciated as such.

At the age of twenty-three, a peculiar thing happened. After receiving some powerful sedative medicine for a headache, Edgar lost the use of his voice. Barely able to speak above a whisper, his then-career as a salesman was in great jeopardy. Doctor after doctor examined him, but to no avail. They regarded Edgar as a medical curiosity, but offered no solutions to his difficulty. Edgar himself recognized that his circumstance was "incurable," that there seemed to be no medical answer forthcoming to his problem.

A traveling hypnotist passed through town and declared that he could cure Edgar by hypnotizing him and making a suggestion to his subconscious mind. During the experiments, Edgar could speak in a normal tone, but the post-hypnotic suggestion did not "take." In his waking state, Edgar was still without a voice. Because the experiment had worked, at least temporarily, a second hypnotist "tried his hand" with Cayce. Again, the results were the same. When a third man suggested an attempt at hypnotism, Edgar's father was not inclined to accept. After all, the previous attempts at hypnotism had proved no more fruitful than the conventional medicine of the time. To Edgar, however, it seemed as if something might be accomplished. A man named Layne taught Edgar how to hypnotize himself or, as he called it, autohypnosis. Cayce followed the instructions and put himself into hypnotic trance. Once in the trance, the hypnotist Layne told Cayce to see his body and describe the trouble in his throat. After a few moments of silence, Edgar began to speak. His words were, "We can see the body." Cayce went on to describe his own physical state. "This body is unable to speak due to a partial paralysis of the interior muscles of the vocal chords produced by nerve strain. This is a psychological condition producing a physical effect. This may be removed by increasing the circulation to the affected parts by suggestion while in this unconscious condition." The hypnotist then gave Cayce the instruction that the circulation would be increased to the affected parts and the condition removed. Everyone was silent as each watched the also-silent Edgar Cayce. They all saw his throat turn pink, then deepen to bright red. After twenty minutes, the color gradually lessened and became normal. Edgar Cayce, still in his hypnotic state, said, "It is all right now. The condition is removed. Make the suggestion that the circulation return to normal and that after that the body awaken."

When the suggestion was given, Cayce returned to normal and awakened. He could talk. The paralysis of his voice had been corrected. Under a self-hypnotic state, he had diagnosed his own difficulty and made the recommendation for his own cure. This was the first discovery of Cayce's true gift.

The book *There Is a River* went on to describe the life and the gifts of Edgar Cayce. Cayce, with his deep religious upbringing, was sometimes afraid of his gift. He, like many of us now, was taught to believe that these kinds of "gifts" were actually works of the devil. His mother, as well as a respected preacher of his time, counseled him differently. "By their fruits ye shall know them," he was taught by those nearest and dearest to him. If the work was one of the devil, it would produce harmful results. The products of Cayce's gifts were beneficial. His information helped people.

For many years he declined to use his gift. It reminded me of Granny, somehow. She, too, had wished that she did not have the gift. Still, when one of Edgar Cayce's young sons was involved in an accident and was told he would lose his sight permanently, Cayce again applied his gift. As a result of the information that he recommended while in his self-induced hypnotic state, his young son recovered his sight. After that, Cayce began to use and respect his special ability.

The book went on to describe the entirety of Cayce's life.

Always a man of modest financial means, Cayce spent most of his life giving what came to be known as "readings" for other people. The majority of the readings, nearly two-thirds, pertained to the physical health of an individual and what could be done to restore it. Cayce also gave "readings" about other topics: spiritual and philosophical matters, earth changes, and other events. An organization currently known as the Association for Research and Enlightenment, Inc. (A.R.E.), was founded to study the readings left by Edgar Cayce.

The story of the life of Edgar Cayce fascinated me. Cayce performed medical diagnoses by clairvoyance for forty-three years. He had no formal medical education. His schooling, except for sleeping on textbooks, ended when he was sixteen years old. Yet his sleep-state diagnostic accuracy was estimated at ninety percent. Reports of 30,000 diagnoses were left to the A.R.E. as well as hundreds of case reports. Written statements and affidavits by patients and reports from their physicians were included with the readings. Many physicians of the time sent their difficult and "incurable" patients to Cayce for diagnosis. Though Cayce had never studied medicine, he was able in over ninety percent of the cases to make a recommendation that proved helpful to the patient.

Though all of this was quite amazing to others, to me, somehow, it was not. Cayce was simply someone else similar to my own grandmother who had a "gift." What was fascinating about Edgar Cayce was the vast number of people whom he had helped with his gift. The recommendations that he made overlapped all segments of the medical community. I read in the book *There Is a River* that someone had once asked, "Tell me this, why does Edgar mix up his treatments so? There are many medicines—allopathic, homeopathic, naturopathic, osteopathic. Edgar seems to use them all. That doesn't make sense."

"I think it does," the questioner was told. "Some people need one form of treatment, some need another. No one school has all the remedies."

The methods recommended by Edgar Cayce knew no boundaries of any particular school of thought. Sometimes Cayce would recommend an herb or a diet. Sometimes his recommendations included osteopathic manipulations or hydrotherapy. All of his recommendations made sense to me. They relied on natural treatments and restoring the body to a normal state. Oftentimes, Cayce suggested that unnatural treatments were correcting symptoms, but not addressing the problem. The cause of the ailment was always addressed in the readings. This, too, seemed logical to me. That, combined with the fact that his recommendations were successful in healing patients, including difficult cases, peaked my interest very greatly. From that age on (twelve), I began to read and study the Cayce readings.

I was not interested in Cayce solely because of his unusual source of information. Neither was I put off by it. After all, it seemed to be the same place that my own grandmother was able to "plug into."

What was most amazing to me was Cayce's philosophy and his results. People who were given up as "incurable" by the conventional doctors of the day often found help from the Cayce readings. No matter what their source, the readings seemed logical and reasonable. If the patient's difficulty had arisen from some deficiency in the diet or from some problem in thought, was it not logical to correct it by the same means? As I finished reading the life story of Edgar Cayce, I became even more inspired by my chosen career goal. Indeed, I wanted to be a doctor. I wanted to be the kind of doctor who used the reasonable treatments that had been so successful from the Cayce readings: correct diet, correct thought, exercise, and natural treatments that would create and restore balance in the system. That seemed rational. That seemed reasonable. It did not seem unusual to me that this reasonable, rational information had been acquired in a "special way." After all, there were others who had had "the gift." Jesus the Christ, the One whom I had always read about because I was a "good Christian girl." My own granny had it, even though Momma said people at church wouldn't understand. Now here was another man, Edgar Cayce, who had "the gift." I studied the Edgar Cayce readings and, in turn, was encouraged in my own studies of medicine. The Edgar Cayce readings helped guide my thinking, no doubt, in the direction of *natural* medicine.

3

THE RECONSIDERATION

From age twelve on, I was both a student of the biological sciences and the Edgar Cayce readings. The two seemed to go hand in hand. In health matters, everything Cayce talked about made very logical sense to me. Instead of merely treating the *symptoms* of a disease, Cayce talked about how to find the cause of disease and correct it.

My thoughts about being a physician grew from there. I envisioned myself being the kind of doctor who would teach people how to take care of themselves. Surely when problems arose, we would look together for the cause. Having found it, we would use the most natural and gentle measures to correct the problems. I always had this in mind when I thought about being a doctor.

True to my mother's word, I was raised as a "good Christian girl." For as long as I could remember, I had been attending the Episcopal church. From second through eighth grade, I went to Catholic school. When I started high school, I began attending a public school. It was then that my parents announced to me that I was old enough to make my own decision as to what church I would attend.

I took this new liberation very seriously. I still didn't understand exactly what the "leap of faith" was. I still wasn't clear on how a God of love that was all powerful would send me to hell for misbehavior. With this in mind, I very carefully attended as many different churches as I could, seeking an answer to my earlier question.

With a Mormon classmate, I went to the Mormon church. They had their own special book, *The Book of Mormon*, which I read from cover to cover. Because my parents had insisted that I take piano and organ lessons from an early age, I was a fairly skilled musician by age twelve. I got a job as an organist at the Christian Science Church. I didn't know anything about Christian Science, but I went to church every Sunday and played the organ and got paid. They, too, had a special book called *Science and Health*, which I read and tried to understand.

I went to the Jewish temple with another friend of mine. I attended nearly every variation of the Protestant religion that was available. I'm sure if there had been a Buddhist temple or any other house of worship in our town, I would have attended that as well. I sincerely wanted to know about this God-being and what I needed to do to be O.K. with Him or Her.

Finally, still at the age of twelve, I settled on a wonderful Presbyterian congregation as my church home. The choir was wonderful. Not only could I sing with the grownups, but they asked me to be their assistant organist. The pastor was a lovely man—what I thought Jesus might have been like when He was on earth. So one day in my twelfth year I became an official member of the Presbyterian Church. My parents proudly attended the ceremony. Several months later they, too, decided to join this church.

As much as I loved my new church, the confusion of my earlier years persisted. Why would an all-loving God send us to eternal damnation if we didn't understand something correctly? Life is admittedly short compared to eternity. Would a God of love punish us to "forever hell" if we didn't "pass the test" in one brief lifetime? And if God was omnipresent, where was hell? How could hell be outside the realm of God?

I studied the Bible. I read where Jesus the Christ said, "I and the Father are one." (John 10:30) And where St. Paul said, "Nothing can ever separate us from the love of God." (Romans 8:30-39) My questions remained: if nothing could separate us from God, where was hell and why would God send us there?

I was still on my path toward being a doctor. Whenever I was given a choice of what to study in school, I always chose the science classes: biology, chemistry, physics, mathematics—I excelled in the sciences.

When I was sixteen, I made another announcement to my parents. "Someday," I told them, "I'm going to work at the A.R.E. Clinic." I didn't know much about the clinic. I had read many books about Edgar Cayce and about Edgar Cayce's healing remedies. Some of the books mentioned a medical clinic in Arizona that used the Cayce remedies. It seemed like an ideal place for me to eventually practice, and I set my sights on it.

Studying the human body was fascinating to me. The body, it seems, had certain requirements rather like a machine. Although it was much more complex than any machine, basic requirements still needed to be met. There was a need for food containing certain nutrients; there was a need for water, for sunlight, for the emotion of caring. All of these things were written about both in the science books and in the Cayce readings. They also were talked about frequently in the Bible. So I read and grew and studied and headed along my path. The path, as I saw it, would be one of doctoring that would help people be healthy.

I graduated a year early from high school, eager to move along with my studies and help people be healthy. From there I began college and declared medical science as my major. With prerequisites of biology, chemistry, and physics to gain entrance to medical school, my first several years of college were exciting and full.

How clearly I remember my first day of Inorganic Chemistry 101. The bald, bearded professor, who looked to be no more than forty years old, stood in front of the class and introduced himself. He announced that he was a Harvard graduate with such authority that I wrote it down. The blackboard was already covered with equations, which he told us was quiz material on Friday. I was scared, but also excited.

In Chemistry 101, I learned more about God than I had in catechism class. Dr. Fowler, the professor, proceeded to tell us about the nature of the material universe. This is what he said: "Everything in the material universe is made out of the *one same thing*—atoms. Atoms are the basic particles out of which everything that is arises. Atoms are comprised of electrical charges and are, therefore, energy. When we 'distill' the universe down to its basic substance, we find that there is no substance. The entire material universe arises out of a nonmaterial universe of energy."

This all sounded so familiar to me. Where had I heard it before? Suddenly I remembered. "Why, it's in the Bible," I reminded myself. "How could that be? This is chemistry class, not Sunday school." My two-way communication with myself continued. After classes that day, I was anxious to get home and look in my own Bible. Sure enough, Chemistry 101 lessons were also found in the Epistle to the Hebrews: "We know the world and the stars—in fact, all things—were made at God's command and that they were all made from things that can't be seen." (Hebrews 11:3)

I puzzled long and hard about this. Could it be that the Unseen Energy (God) becomes all material things? I thumbed further through the Bible until my eyes fell on a sentence that I had underlined years earlier: "He created everything there is—nothing exists that He didn't make." (John 1:3)

I could still hear the professor's words from the morning class: "Everything . . . is made out of the *one same thing . . .* " My excitement grew.

The following day I attended my first physics class. Among other things, we learned about the second law of thermodynamics. This scientific law says that energy cannot be created or destroyed by ordinary means; it can only be changed in form.

I reflected back to my religious training. We were always taught in church, Sunday school, and Catholic school that there is an afterlife. A soul does not die upon death of the body. Like the day before, I was eager to dash home and look in my Bible.

After I leafed through its pages, my thoughts went something like this, as I remember back: When we are alive, there is an energy that animates the body. It is the *life* within us. At death, the body still looks the same, except that the *life* (energy) is gone. In physics class, we had just learned that energy cannot be destroyed, but can only be changed in form. The energy that gives our body *life* cannot simply cease to be at death. That would contradict the second law of thermodynamics. It would also contradict what I was taught from the Bible. My Sunday school teacher, my pastor, and my physics professor all seemed to agree on this point of *life* after death, though they didn't necessarily know of their agreement! My eyes fell on a highlighted paragraph in my Bible: "For our earthly bodies, the ones we have now that can die, must be transformed into heavenly bodies that cannot perish but will live forever." (I Corinthians 15:53) "This is religion," I thought, "but it's also science. Energy cannot be destroyed . . . only changed in form."

Biology was my favorite subject. The complexity of both human and animal organisms awed me. If there was any doubt in my mind as to the existence of the Supreme Being, it was erased when I studied biology in college. The laws of the nature of chemistry, physics, and biology are so precise and so complex. How could there not be a Divine Source behind them? I was always amused at those scientists who would say there is no God. If any one of us walked into an empty room and saw a typewriter with a written manuscript in the carriage, we would believe that an intelligent life had been there first. It would not occur to us that creation had arisen spontaneously or by accident. We would know with certainty someone with intelligence had been there to create it. How much more complex is this phenomenon we call life! Why would we think for an instance that it had no divine, creative, intelligent Source behind it? Though I still didn't understand the nature of the Supreme Being or the laws that the Sunday school teachers and the preachers were trying to teach me in church, I was certain of this: there is an intelligent Source that underlies creation. My frustration of not having an answer to the "leap of faith" persisted. I was comforted by the fact that I was certain of that Intelligence, however.

In my third and fourth year of college I was finally into the classes that pertained to medicine. One day in a medical ethics class the teacher asked us to answer anonymously one question. We were to put in order of priority our reasons for going into medicine. When the answers were tallied, the teacher wrote them on the board. "Money" was

number one, "respect" was number two, "the desire to help
people" was number three. I was crestfallen. As I looked
around the class, I saw my future medical colleagues. The
numbers our class came up with frightened and saddened
me.

I was still a student of the Cayce readings. The many healing therapies mentioned by Cayce included nutrition,
spinal manipulation, hydrotherapy, massage, and herbs. As
I got closer to entering medical school, I realized I would
not be taught any of those sciences. Instead, I would be
taught how to use chemicals and surgery to treat the apparent symptoms of the disease. I felt some confusion about
this, but, like the "leap of faith," I put it aside.

Like all good pre-med students, I "did all the right things."
I volunteered at one hospital as an assistant to the pathologist. At another, I was a research assistant to the chief of
neurosurgery. Extracurricular activities like these were sure
to gain me a seat in medical school.

The chief with whom I worked was a very dedicated man.
He had developed revolutionary techniques for back surgery. He also had developed the surgical instruments
necessary to perform the surgery. Not only was he brilliant,
he was very wealthy.

He was so conscientious with his work that he refused to
drink any coffee. "How would I feel," he asked me, "if my
hand trembled one day during surgery and I lost a patient
because of that tremble? If I knew that the tremble might
have even *remotely* been caused by a choice I made, like
drinking coffee, I could not, would not, forgive myself." His
philosophy was to take excellent care of his body on behalf
of the patients he served. I greatly respected him.

In discussing the surgical techniques and instruments he
devised, he always sounded amazed at his success. It
seemed so logical, so simple, he told me. He couldn't believe that someone else hadn't thought of it first. As simple

as he believed this technique to be, it shortened the time of recovery from back surgery from two weeks to two days. To him it was easy.

Because he was the chief of neurosurgery, he would get a weekly report from the hospital. I remember one day passing the open door to his office and seeing him bang his fist on the desk and say, "Damn!"

"Dr. G.," I said meekly, "what is the matter?"

"Oh, this," he said, tossing a computer printout at me. The paper showed percent occupancy in each of the departments of the hospital. I had seen the reports before, many times. The reports were designed to show the chiefs of staff what percentage of beds were full in their departments of the hospital. We all knew why the reports were made. There was a "percent occupancy" that was expected in each of the departments. Neurosurgery, being a specialty, was less than the others at sixty percent. This report showed forty percent, and it was highlighted with red ink.

"What do they expect me to do?" he shouted, not to me, but just in general. "Perform more brain surgery to keep the beds full?" He slammed his fist on the desk again. Somehow I knew I dare not say anything, not even in consolation. I looked at the report, delicately placed it on his desk, and left his office.

Then there was Millie. Millie came into the hospital having suffered a stroke. Her personality and enthusiasm for life were contagious. Everyone who knew her or worked with her always left her room smiling. I had seen her because she was there for her neurological consult.

The real problem with Millie was that she had atherosclerotic disease. This means the arteries in her body contained deposits of fat. A small piece of the fat had broken loose and gone to her brain which had caused a stroke. Even more worrisome were the blockages in the vessels of her heart. Tests revealed that she was also at risk for having a heart attack. At the time, however, she was having no symptoms.

Millie was a delight to visit, and I would stop in every day that I was at the hospital. In talking to her, I found out that she had adult-onset diabetes. Though she used insulin, her blood sugar was still very high. Although someone had mentioned the importance of diet to her, she had never been counseled about dietary procedure. She was totally surprised to hear that exercise helps lower blood sugar levels. From looking at her records and from her story, it sounded to me like Millie's diabetes would be reversible through diet, exercise, and careful insulin control. This came as a great surprise to Millie, and she was eager to hear what I had to say.

Armed with nutritional information from my college studies and from the Cayce readings, I devised a diet and exercise program that I was certain would help reverse Millie's diabetes. Since diabetes can cause atherosclerosis, correcting the diabetes would be the first step in correcting the secondary problems that she had.

Millie never had the chance to try the diet that I painstakingly prepared for her. Doctors in the hospital told her that without coronary by-pass surgery, she would die. Surely she knew, and so did they, that she would die some day of something. Millie thought from her conversation with the doctors that her by-pass surgery would prolong her life. Statistically speaking, there is no basis for this belief. The numbers show that by-pass surgery *does not prolong the life* of someone with coronary vascular disease. Statistics also show that dietary changes can have long-lasting and genuine effects. Before I had the opportunity to tell Millie, she was whisked away to surgery. She had the surgery, suffered a severe stroke, and never recovered. Millie never regained consciousness before she died.

I frustrated some of my college professors much as I had

Father O'Connor in Catholic school. When they taught us to treat infection with antibiotics, I wanted to know why a body would get an infection. The answer, I was told, was simple. Bacteria caused infection. Antibiotics kill bacteria. Therefore, antibiotics cured infections.

The same emotions that I felt when I wanted to know about hell and where it was and why God would send us there came flooding over me. "Bacteria is everywhere," I challenged the professors. "We are all exposed to them. Why do some people get sick and others not?" I demanded to know.

"Well," said one professor thoughtfully, "it has to do with the state of the person's own immune system. Obviously, if a person's immune system is not up to par, that person is susceptible to disease."

"Well, then," I countered, "how come we don't talk about how to strengthen the immune system instead of just how to kill the bug?" When the professor stared at me and I stared at him, it was déjà vu. He had no answer.

If unanswered questions about God had frustrated me as a child, unanswered questions about medicine frustrated me as a young adult. Why were we treating symptoms instead of causes, I wanted to know. The answer was just about the same as it had been with earlier questions: "Leap of faith. This is just the way it's done."

One night I was at a rare party comprised mostly of the doctors at the hospital. There were very few students present. I was there only because I worked as a research assistant to two different chiefs of staff. Most of the doctors at the party were men. Indoors they were watching off-color movies and drinking beer. Recognizing this as an opportunity to rub elbows with the people who would recommend me for medical school, I was hesitant to leave. I stepped outside to catch a breath of fresh air, and it was there that I saw Dr. Horner standing by his car.

Dr. Horner was the chief of cardiology at the same hospital where I volunteered. He was pretty drunk, standing over his Ferrari sports car, crying. With genuine concern, I approached him and said "What's the matter?" His tale changed my life forever.

"Well," he said, in his slurred voice, "I feel awful about the work I do."

"What do you mean?" I asked. I expected his answer to come more from his drunkenness than from reason.

"I hate it when I get those percent occupancy reports," he slammed his fist on the car. "What am I supposed to do? Perform heart surgeries when they're not needed to keep the percent occupancy up? Yes!" he answered his own question and slammed his fist again.

"Well, if you don't like it," I reasoned, "why don't you leave the hospital?"

"Oh, yeah, right," he said sarcastically. "And then what would I do? I'm trained as a surgeon. A surgeon has to operate. Whether I'm the chief of a department or just a staff surgeon, I have to operate to make a living; and it doesn't matter where I go, I'll have to do the same thing. I'm stuck."

Something inside me snapped. I can't explain it, only to say that I couldn't catch my breath. I was in shock, in horror. Not from what I had just heard. I already knew that. I had already seen that. It was more from what I had just realized. I could not be a doctor. Not if being a doctor meant that I treated symptoms instead of causes. Not if it meant that percent occupancies and bottom lines were more important than getting patients better. His words went through my heart like a knife. Being a doctor, at least like this, was not what I had envisioned. It was not what seemed reasonable. I went into the house, grabbed my coat, said my good-bys, and left quickly. I felt as if a close family member had suddenly been killed in an unexpected accident. Part of me died that night. The part that wanted to be a physician.

4

THE ROAD NOT TAKEN

For days after the party, I grieved. There are few times in my life when I remember feeling so sad. When Grandma died, I felt unspeakably sad. I felt like that again. To have loved something, to have wanted something for so long, and to suddenly feel that it was taken away. The grief was like losing a dear one to death.

How could I possibly tell my parents that I had changed my mind about being a doctor? The only thing they had ever heard me say since I was eight years old was that I wanted to be a doctor when I grew up. Half of my allowance was lovingly saved every week toward my medical school tuition fund. I lived it, I breathed it, I studied it from an early age. Now, I no longer wanted it. How could I possibly tell them that I had changed my mind?

I decided that I would think about it for a few days before I made my announcement. It has always been my way to consider things from every angle before making a decision. There was no denying the great benefit to be gained from the medicine that I was studying.

Had I not seen a miraculous bit of micro-neurosurgery save the life of a seventeen-year-old? Using overhead microscopes that allowed him to observe the delicate portions of the brain, Dr. Harold had performed an intricate tumor removal. I had been there in the surgical suite. I saw what he was seeing on the overhead closed-circuit TV. It was miraculous. I had seen a young man brought back from the brink of death by this masterpiece of technology and human courage. Removal of a tumor of this sort would not have been possible without the benefits of modern medicine. I had been there . . . I saw . . . I knew.

I had been there, too, for a remarkable autopsy with pathologist Dr. Ramos. Inspecting the body of a two-year-old who was thought to have died of sudden infant death syndrome, Dr. Ramos determined that her death had been caused by suffocation. With delicate exploration of lung tissue conducted under a microscope, Dr. Ramos determined that the baby's death was not accidental. Once Dr. Ramos stated his findings, the father came forth and admitted that he had suffocated the little girl. The man was brought to justice for his crime. This never could have happened without the advances, skill, and technology of modern medical science.

On the other hand, I remembered Millie. Millie was not the only person, but certainly the most memorable, whom I had known to die of cardiovascular disease. No one had told her that her condition was highly treatable through correction of diet and life style. She had been led to believe that her only alternative was technology. Because she believed that and knew no other choice, she took it. And now,

Millie was gone. She had suffered a stroke during by-pass surgery.

I remembered Mrs. Morgan, another lady, who came in with a urinary tract infection. The CAT scan showed a mass in one of the arteries that supplies the kidney. When further tests were conducted by injecting dye into the vessels of her kidney, she suffered a serious stroke. The tests revealed that the mass was benign. It would not have caused any problem. The *test* is what caused the problem. "Did the benefit of being able to look more closely outweigh the harm it caused the patient?" I wondered to myself. "And where did the line go?"

Then there were the patients whom I had seen enter our hospital; the ones who came in with non-life-threatening diseases. Sometimes we knew how to treat them and sometimes we did not. Many times our treatments were more dangerous than the disease. I remembered those times when I felt like taking the patients aside and whispering in their ear, "Look, get out now, trust me . . . just leave, before we do anything to you, because your illness will not hurt as much as our treatment for it." I never said those things to anyone, but there were times when I felt like doing that.

Did we demand, and sternly enough, that our patients stop smoking? No. We waited until they had lung cancer, then we applied our feeble treatments. We all knew that when someone had a diagnosis of lung cancer, there was very little that our conventional medicine could provide.

When patients came to us with high blood pressure and at risk for stroke or heart attack, did we teach and encourage them to change their diet and to exercise? No. We gave them medicine for their blood pressure and waited. Then, when they had the heart attack, we treated them in our intensive care unit and recommended by-pass surgery for their clogged arteries. Why did we do it that way, when we knew a better way? The questions were too confusing.

In weighing my decision about medical school, I returned again to the Edgar Cayce readings for help and
inspiration. Cayce said that there were no incurable diseases . . . only incurable people. This I believed because I
had seen it with my own eyes in the hospitals. Though not
necessarily the rule, there were always those folks who had
recovered from "incurable illnesses." The readings were so
simple. Yet in their simplicity was a scientific elegance. The
body has certain basic requirements to function well. Give
it what it needs. The body recognizes certain things as being detrimental. These things will cause harm in the body.
Discontinue them. Our mind, our thoughts, and our emotions can change the nervous and the endocrine systems.
Therefore, thoughts are important in terms of health and
disease. Be certain that your thoughts are moving you in
the direction of health, if that is where you mean to go.

These basic and simple steps from the Cayce readings
were consistent with everything I had learned in science.
The body has certain nutritional requirements and, if they
are not met, the body will suffer. We know there are some
things that irritate and aggravate the body. If we do them
consistently, we will create injury to the body. This was not
mysterious. This was not some esoteric belief given by a
psychic. This information was simple logic and basic understanding. Why did I feel so alone in my recognition of
these facts? Was I missing something again, like I did in second grade with Father O'Connor?

After several days of deliberation, I reached my conclu-
sion. It was entirely true, I knew, that miracles were sometimes
wrought by modern medical technology. The thought
crossed my mind to continue on in medicine as a specialist,
one like Dr. Harold who performed delicate micro-surgical
techniques. But I knew I didn't want to be a specialist. I
wanted to be a family doctor. The one who delivers the ba-
bies and treats the toddler and mom and dad and grand-

parents. Though there was much from technological medicine that could help, there was much, I felt, that could not. In many instances, not only were the treatments I would learn in medical school useless, many were actually harmful. Treating someone for cardiovascular disease with drugs instead of first correcting the diet flew in the face of everything I understood to be correct. I also recognized another thing: I had always thought that I would be a doctor . . . a family practitioner who would treat people by logical and natural methods. The natural methods that I had in mind were founded in science and reinforced from the readings of Edgar Cayce. Looking at catalogs from all the medical schools that I had collected, I realized that I would learn nothing of the sorts of therapies that I had intended to know about. After graduating from medical school, I would be a technologist, someone who understood drugs and surgery and the high-tech machinery which has its place. Where were the nutrition, hydrotherapy, exercise physiology, correctness of thought, massage, and spinal manipulation that also had their place? Where were the tools that I would use more often in general family practice? I would not be taught these things in medical school. I would graduate having learned a lot about the tools I didn't want to use and having learned nothing about the tools that I would need most often.

My decision became clear. In the fourth year of my premedical studies in college, I called my parents and made my pronouncement. "Hello, Mom?" My voice was quavering. "Is Dad on the line, too?" I heard them both bark a cheerful, "Yes." They were both listening. "Uh, I have something to tell you," I said, feeling a wave of nausea in the pit of my stomach. "I've decided that, well, I've changed my mind. I don't want to be a doctor after all."

Silence. A longer silence than when I asked Father O'Connor where hell was and why would God send us there. Then I heard my mother ask a fearful, almost tearful,

"Why?"

"Mom, I'm sorry. It's just that being a doctor isn't what I thought it was going to be. I thought I was going to be helping people stay well. I thought I was going to be helping them find the cause of their illness when they got sick. Some of it is like that . . . but so much of it isn't. I wanted to be able to teach people how to live, not wait until they were sick to figure out how to put a patch on them."

Then my dad spoke up, "Sweetheart, you know your mother and I have always wanted you to do whatever you want to do. But you've always wanted to be a doctor." He reminded me as if I'd forgotten that myself. "Maybe you're just not thinking clearly about this right now."

"You don't understand," I argued. "Did you ever read a book I sent you called *Confessions of a Medical Heretic* by Robert Mendelson?" I heard "Uh, huhs" on the other end of the line indicating that they had. "Well," I went on, "for all the good that modern medicine does, there are a lot of abuses. I've been on the inside, I've seen it. You just wouldn't believe it if I told you," I said. "I couldn't even try."

"So what will you do if you don't go to medical school?" my mother asked.

"I don't know. Join the circus maybe," I said, trying to lighten the conversation. I had no idea what I would do if I wasn't a doctor. It was the only thing I had ever wanted to be, and now I didn't want to be it.

"O.K., honey, we'll talk to you later," my mother said. We bid our good-bys and hung up for the night. "What would I do?" I wondered. Something to do with science, I supposed, and yet there was really nothing else I was interested in.

Days passed. I talked to different people in that period of time. One of them was my family dentist. When he heard that I didn't want to go to conventional medical school, he gave me his best advice. "Go to *real* medical school first," he counseled, "then you can go off and do whatever other thing you want to do." It was hard to argue with his logic, with his hands in my mouth. I thought to myself, "Yes, but where will I learn these 'other things' that I want to do if someone doesn't teach me in medical school? Will I be a 'real doctor' and then spend the rest of my life taking weekend courses in things like acupuncture and herbology? That ought to make me an expert in such topics in about another 100 years." And so went the advice that came from well-meaning friends and family.

In the back of a *Prevention* magazine, my mother saw a three-line advertisement which read:

Be a Doctor of Naturopathic Medicine
Four-year degree granted
Accredited

She didn't know anything about naturopathic medicine. When I asked her later, she said she really didn't know what it was, but thought it might be closer to what I was talking about. She sent my name to the school and had a catalog sent to my address.

A manila envelope came to me in the mail one day. Inside was a catalog from a naturopathic medical school. The catalog looked professional, like the other medical school catalogs I'd read. The inside was different, however. It described a four-year medical program with all of the basic sciences, all of the classes in diagnosis and laboratory medicine and therapeutics. Then it went on describing classes in nutrition, herbal medicine, manipulation, hydrotherapy, homeopathy, and Chinese medicine. All of these, with the exception of Chinese medicine, were therapies I had read about in the Cayce readings. It sounded too good to be true. I was skeptical. I finished reading the catalog, then went to the library to do some research. I telephoned my medical advisor and asked what she knew about this. As the story of naturopathic medicine unfolded before me, I dared to believe again that I might be a physician.

5

ANOTHER KIND OF DOCTOR

It's easy to criticize something that we don't understand. Labels allow us to make judgments without having to take the time to really *know.* Some people spoke disparagingly about naturopathic medicine, without even knowing what it really was. I mentioned naturopathic medicine to my family dentist; he counseled me to go to "real medical school first. Then you can go off and do this other thing." When I questioned him further, he admitted that he actually had never heard of naturopathy and, therefore, assumed it couldn't be a "real science."

Because I had decided that I no longer wanted to be a "regular" doctor, I had nothing to lose by finding out about naturopathy. As part of my search for answers, I went to visit the only two fully accredited naturopathic medical colleges in the United States. I wanted to see for myself what they were like and what the students were like.

There are many ways to practice the healing arts. Many very good practitioners are self-taught. I've met folks who do acupressure and reflexology, people who give good nutritional advice or work with energy medicine, and some of them are very skillful. There is something about the term "doctor" that implies a certain level of knowledge, however. We expect that a family physician would recognize if our chest pain was a heart attack or gastric indigestion. My concern was, "Would I be a general practitioner, able to fulfill the duties of a 'doctor,' if I went to this school?" When I arrived in Portland, Oregon, I went to the National College of Naturopathic Medicine and stood in the hallway. I watched the students going by. They looked happy—enjoying what they were doing. I spoke to some and introduced myself. In a short period of time, I met students who had chosen naturopathic medicine as their first career. I also met students who had chosen it as their *second* career. There was a medical doctor, a dentist, a Ph.D. biochemist, several laboratory technicians, and a number of nurses. These folks were all interested in medicine and the complementary methods of healing. I was encouraged to see so many intelligent people among the student population of the school. Surely if this program were a hoax, it would not have attracted people of this caliber.

As I talked to the students and met with the dean of the school, a picture of naturopathy began to emerge for me. This is what I found. Envision a physician who has been through the usual rigors of medical school: four years of premedical studies followed by four years of medical school; a physician trained in the traditional methods of diagnosis and treatment: laboratory medicine, pathology, physical examination, pharmacology, minor surgery. Now envision that this physician has also received training in complementary medicine: nutrition, herbal medicine, homeopathy, manipulation, and Chinese medicine, while still in medical school. If you can conceive of such a physician, then you understand the discipline of naturopathic medicine.

I found that naturopaths were trained as primary care physicians—taught to perform physical examinations, well-baby checks, gynecological exams, and all matters of general family care. Some naturopathic physicians also do obstetrics.

Philosophically, naturopathic physicians believe that the human body is a self-repairing organism when given the proper circumstances. Instead of being trained to treat a *symptom*, naturopathic doctors are trained to treat the *person who has the symptom*.

No one to whom I talked would deny that drugs and surgery could be helpful and even lifesaving. Naturopaths will administer, prescribe, or refer for these treatments when they appear to be necessary. As a first line of treatment, however, the naturopathic physician is more likely to recommend a diet change, an herb, a homeopathic remedy, or some other natural remedy to restore balance and health.

The prerequisite training for naturopathic medical school is the same as for conventional medical school. Basic biological sciences—biochemistry, anatomy, physiology, histology—are the same. In addition to the conventional body of knowledge, naturopaths must also take classes in natural therapeutics and diagnosis. Because of this additional training, I discovered that the four-year naturopathic curriculum has more hours of classroom course work than the curriculum in most conventional medical schools.

In my mind, there were still unanswered questions. If naturopaths had a similar level of training and background as any other family physician, why were they not more well known or recognized? As I searched for the answer to this question, another picture began to emerge.

Once upon a time, in the early 1900s, the value of natural and preventive treatments was well recognized and appreciated. Natural therapeutics were taught extensively in every major medical school in the country. There was no standardization of medical schools at that time, however. The medical profession itself was met with much criticism for this lack of standardization. In 1920, a physician named Flexner examined the profession of medicine. He filed a report now widely known as the Flexner Report. In this document, Flexner exposed the great degree of variability among training of physicians of the time. It was decided among the medical profession that standardization of medical schools would be necessary to insure solid public acceptance. A direction had to be taken for the entire profession. Because chemical medicine was coming into popularity and, with the growing support of the pharmaceutical companies, a direction for medicine was decided. Medical schools would teach a standard curriculum that would focus on treatment with drugs and surgery. Classes in natural therapeutics were systematically removed from the curriculum. Again, this was not because these subjects were thought to be ineffective; it was simply that medicine had to decide on one particular direction in order to maintain credibility. At that time, and with the political influence and pressure of the budding pharmaceutical industry, a particular direction was chosen because it was thought to be more politically advantageous.

Where classes in natural therapies had once been taught in medical schools, they were removed. Doctors were trained in pharmacology and surgery, and the population was taught that this was the superior method of healing.

One amusing thing I found in my research is the definition of a "drug" versus an "herb." Modern medicine has a tendency to downplay the effectiveness of herbal medicine, saying that it hasn't been proved or found to be effective. In truth, some forty percent of all our modern-day drugs are derived directly from plant sources: digitalis from the plant foxglove; antibiotics from various strains of fungi; progesterone from the wild yam plant. Even many of the synthetic drugs were first discovered from a plant source. After "their" discovery, drug companies try to find ways to synthetically make the same chemical, but much of our modern-day pharmacy is still derived directly from herbs.

The more I researched, the more fascinated I became with naturopathic medicine. The study of the human body and the natural correction of disease is older than our modern-day medicine. In fact, it was a part of our modern medicine until, for political reasons, it was decided that it was disadvantageous. At no time could I find evidence that the natural methods of healing were proved ineffective. In fact, there is much information in the scientific literature today which validates and verifies the practices and principles used by naturopathic physicians.

My next question was more practical, a matter of self-preservation. Were naturopathic physicians licensed by states, like medical doctors or osteopathic doctors or chiropractors? The answer was yes and no. Some states have naturopathic licensing boards which examine the qualifications of physicians and grant licenses. Other states do not, yet have licensing laws in place for naturopaths. "Why do some states not have licensing laws?" I wanted to know. The answers, while simple, are severalfold. First, naturopaths are far fewer in number than other types of physicians. This is probably because there are only two accredited naturopathic medical schools and because of the great political challenge placed on naturopaths to practice. A naturopathic doctor cannot simply be a physician, but he or she must also be politically active in defending the profession. It's a steep challenge. Many who would otherwise enjoy the practice of naturopathy find the challenges too great. In contrast to the hundreds of thousands of licensed M.D.s in this country, there are less than 2,000 actively practicing naturopathic physicians. Now, envision the "catch-22" at the level of state licensing. It is much easier and more comfortable to practice naturopathic medicine in a state where you are licensed. The risk of being hassled for "practicing medicine without a license" is reduced to zero. By contrast, practicing in a nonlicensed state means potentially being harassed for "practicing medicine without a license." Never mind the fact that the state may not *have* a mechanism to license a naturopathic physician; that's just the way the politics go. For this reason, many qualified naturopaths prefer to go to states that already have licensing laws in place. If physicians go to a nonlicensed state, they may be challenged for practicing medicine without a license. The state, in turn, is not likely to establish a board of medical examiners for a nonexistent profession. A state will not bother to establish a medical licensing board for naturopaths if there aren't any practicing naturopaths in the state. In fact, it's not even financially feasible to a state to establish a licensing board until the numbers of naturopaths are quite a bit larger in that state. States don't want to license naturopaths until there's enough of them to make it financially feasible, and naturopaths don't want to go to states where there is no licensing. The "catch-22." In spite of this challenge, there are naturopaths practicing in nearly every state. Until the numbers are greater, many states will remain nonlicensed.

The second challenge exists from outside the profession. Other professions, particularly the conventional medical profession, e.g., M.D.s, have a strong lobby effort. Again, it is easy to label and criticize what we do not understand. Many local branches of the AMA, not really knowing or understanding what a naturopath is, will automatically campaign against the profession. Without knowing the sound, scientific basis for our profession, without knowing that we graduate from four-year programs that are federally accredited, many will criticize and lobby against us. Their lobby is strong. Couple that with the fact that in many parts of the country, legislators do not know what the qualifications of a naturopathic physician are. So, if you don't know what a naturopath is and someone comes along whom you respect and offers you an opinion, what else are you to think? A challenge, to be sure, not only for the naturopathic profession, but for the lay public who would like to have the freedom to chose a naturopathic physician for their family doctor.

After examining the evidence, after searching broadly and deeply, I decided that being a naturopathic physician was more like what I'd had in mind all along. I recognized that there would be political challenges, both at the state level of licensing and at an individual level. On the other hand, I also recognized that my years in naturopathic medical school would train me to be the kind of physician I had always envisioned being—one who was qualified to practice general family medicine and who could perform diagnoses on the level agreed upon as being the "standard of care." I also recognized that I would be able to look at the body in other ways in addition to my conventional training. I would be able to look at the body and consider it a masterpiece of design—able, in many circumstances, to heal itself when given proper conditions. I would not be limited to treating symptoms, but could instead look for the causes of symptoms. And, upon graduation, I would be skilled in many of the methods and remedies that have been an historical part of medicine since the dawn of time.

I graduated from my state university with a bachelor's degree in medical science. Also, true to my mother's promise to God, I was a "good Christian girl," well versed in Scripture and the teachings of the Christian church.

Before making my final decision about naturopathic medical school, I decided to take a personal journey. With a friend, I bicycled across the United States, then flew to Europe where we spent four months bicycling through various countries. The interpersonal experiences were wonderful ... the memories will last me a lifetime. And, I found out more about my chosen profession as I traveled.

In Europe, natural therapies such as herbalism and homeopathy are widely used and respected. In fact, many medical physicians practice their herbal therapies and natural treatments along with everything else they do. In other words, the medical physicians in Europe are trained in a way that is quite similar to naturopathic medicine. There are many naturopaths in most European countries. The large pharmaceutical houses in Europe are the same companies that produce the homeopathic and herbal medicines.

I had a touch of upper respiratory tract infection while on the trip. A woman in Holland ran to the local pharmacy to purchase an herbal remedy. It did the job, and I was back on my bicycle trip in short order.

We found another treatment, "taking the waters," that is highly regarded in Europe. Although most of us have never heard of it in this country, it has always been a part of naturopathic therapeutics. High blood pressure, which is often related to overweight and stress, is treated very differently in many European countries. Once a year, for a period of one to three weeks, busy executives and working-class members go away to a health spa for treatment. There, they eat a nutritious diet, sit in the hot mineral waters of local springs, learn relaxation techniques, and commune with nature. This treatment is highly effective in preventing and reversing high blood pressure. We know for a fact from the scientific literature that obesity, faulty diet, and stress can cause this problem. Instead of doctors simply giving a medication to change the way the blood vessels or the kidneys perform, a spa is the European first line of therapy.

If our country were doing better than anyone else in the world, we might disregard the treatments of others and their thoughts about healing. The truth is that the United States ranks sixth in terms of mean average life span after age forty. This means that there are five other countries that do better than we do in terms of their health care. In terms of the amount of money we spend for health care, we are number one! Doesn't it seem that, for all our technology and the amount of money we're spending, we should have the best health care in the world? The statistics do not verify that we do. Perhaps there is something that we can learn from other countries that are healthier and wealthier than ourselves.

Long hours on the road on a bicycle provided plenty of time to think. It gave me an opportunity to weigh everything I knew and that I thought I knew in making my final decision. On the one hand, I would be the last to deny the benefits and miracles of modern medicine. I had seen healing miracles wrought through surgery and lives saved through chemistry. It did not, however, seem to me to provide the only answer or the consistently best answer.

There were times when the high tech was not the best tech; times when performing surgery or giving drugs made little sense. I likened what I had seen on some occasions to a fly on the wall. A fly on the wall, if it is an annoyance that needs to be destroyed, requires a fly swatter. If you take out a cannon to destroy the fly, you may destroy the fly and the wall together. A cannon is far more treatment than you need for a small annoyance like a fly. In some circumstances, the cannon would be your best answer. In other circumstances, the cannon makes no sense. Why, I wondered, didn't many of the brilliant men and women of science, on either side of the issue, recognize this? Why was it not more widely appreciated? At times what is reasonable and helpful is at other times unreasonable and harmful. Why wouldn't these issues be examined so that the best answer could be discovered? Again, it seemed to me that the answer lies in politics. We are taught to think in black and white. If it's black, it can't be white; if it's white, it can't be black. When we fail to consider the infinite number of shades of gray in between black and white, we polarize our thinking. Brilliant minds get locked into a box and fail to appreciate the bigger picture. Although I understood and greatly valued the many benefits to be had from conventional medicine, I still determined that for most of my general family practice, it was not the most serviceable knowledge for me to have. I needed a more complete knowledge, one that included both the conventional *and* the natural methods. If I understood how to be a good generalist, how to help reverse disease in its early stages through the least invasive methods, I would not often require the "cannon" of modern medicine. At those times when the "big gun"—the heroic treatment—was the best answer, I would be well qualified to make a referral. As a general practitioner, and one inspired by natural good sense and observation and by the Cayce readings, I determined that the naturopathic curriculum was better suited to my needs. When I returned home, I applied to and was accepted by the National College of Naturopathic Medicine.

6

THE MAKING OF A PHYSICIAN

Excitement flowed like electricity through the classroom on that first day. As we each sat gazing at a room full of strangers, we could feel the potential in the air. A young well-dressed man appeared and walked to the front of the room. Introducing himself as Dr. Bennett, he said he would be guiding us through the procedures and protocols of our first week of classes. He would also be instructing us in clinical and physical diagnosis in our second year of studies.

"Before we proceed further," he began, "I'd like us to introduce ourselves to each other. Take a moment to look at the other faces that surround you. Though you're all strangers now, very soon these people will be your family. You will be studying with them. You will be eating many of your meals together. You will be learning everything from anatomy to physical diagnosis together. You will be sharing all the joys, sorrows, and other experiences of medical school together. Look around. Over the course of the next four years, this group of faces will become your other family."

At his suggestion we gazed more openly at each other. I was amazed to see the great diversity of people sitting in the room. There was one young man who wore a turban. There were several people with dark skins. They looked East Indian to me. There were young folks and old folks. There were all sizes and shapes. In fact, this room full of people, though it numbered around forty, looked to be one of the most diverse groups I had ever seen. I stared in wonderment at my new "family."

Dr. Bennett went on to explain: "In some medical schools," he paused until we were all attentive, "models are hired to help you learn your physical examination skills. In *this* medical school, we do it differently. As you learn to listen, observe, hear, and feel the sounds, sights, and sensations of the human body, you will be practicing your examination skills on each other." He paused again, giving us time to understand the meaning of his words. Finally, a hand went up in the back of the room.

"Does that mean that we will be doing GYN exams on each other?" a female voice inquired meekly.

"You will be practicing every type of examination on each other," he said slowly and with emphasis. "We must all learn to do female examinations. The women in our class will be the models. We must all learn to do male examinations, including the prostate. The males in our class will be the models for the rest of the class. You will learn to look in eyes, ears, and throats on each other. You will learn to appreciate heart sounds and palpate the abdomen on each other. You will learn to draw blood, perform minor surgery, and catheterize urinary bladders on each other." The class was silent as we contemplated his words.

The term "family" suddenly took on new meaning for me. *Of course*, these people would become "family." Not only would we go through the trials and tribulations of medical school together, but we would be intimately familiar with everyone's anatomy. The silence continued . . . prolonged. "I'm not going to do it; they can't make me," I heard someone whisper quietly behind me. There may be several people, I thought to myself, who will decide today that they don't want to be physicians after all!

Dr. Bennett proceeded without further hesitation or emphasis. "There will be various study groups and extracurricular organizations that you may join. We will have people here to introduce you to those opportunities this morning. Some of you have asked about the possibility of working at a part-time job outside of school. Although some have done it and it is possible, I do not advise it. You will find your studies to be a full-time job. Be sure to remember to make sufficient time to take care of yourselves. You are learning to treat other people through a means that is natural and wholesome. Begin now to practice what you will be teaching.

"There will be opportunities at 7:00 a.m. in the morning to meet for T'ai Chi or yoga. Classes begin at 8:00 a.m. The professors will not wait for you if you are late. Do not ask them to repeat information that you have missed. This is unfair to your classmates and slows down the learning process.

"You will want to be sure that your microscopes are in working order. Masks and plastic gloves for anatomy can be purchased in the bookstore. If you have personal difficulties or questions, please direct them to the Dean of Student Services. She will be able to help you get settled in your new home. I wish you all the best of success in your course of studies. You have chosen one of the oldest and most profound healing professions. May you all live up to the reputation of this high calling."

Without asking for further questions, he turned and left the room. Again we sat silent in a roomful of strangers, contemplating the information we had just been given.

Another young woman came in shortly after Dr. Bennett's exit. She introduced herself and proceeded to invite us to a meeting pertaining to the politics of our profession. She explained that there was much work to be done, politically speaking, within the field of naturopathy. Because allopathic medicine had held the monopoly on healing in this country for so many years, naturopaths must be politically active to defend their right to practice healing. I instantly recognized the legitimacy of her words. "After I'm finished speaking, please come and introduce yourselves to me if you are interested in participating in political activities within the profession." Just after her talk, I and one other student in the room approached her simultaneously. My eyes locked with my classmate's. We smiled. There was something different about her, I could tell. As we each in turn extended our hand to meet the doctor, I heard her name.

"Louise," she said. "Most people call me Lou."

"Lou," I thought to myself with a smile—what a great name for a study partner. Somehow, in that moment I knew that Louise and I would be study buddies in school. It was rapport at first meeting. I wondered if Lou felt it, too?

So much came to us that first day that we were all fairly quiet in contemplation.

In addition to thinking about the difficulty of my upcoming studies, I had another concern. "What about my classmates?" I wondered and perhaps even spoke the words out loud as I walked to my house several blocks away. From

my many years of upbringing as a "good Christian girl," I
had been taught one thing consistently: there was one way
to believe and only, basically, one way. If someone did not
believe in that particular way, that person would go to hell.
I had been trained in church and at school that it was my
responsibility as a Christian to convert others to my way of
thinking. It didn't matter that I was still unclear about my
own way of thinking. It didn't matter that my questions were
still unanswered about how a loving God could send one to
hell. No matter my questions, I must convert others to my
faith. What I had been told was this: if someone is a non-
Christian, either convert that individual to Christianity or
ignore him or her. Until this day I had never given much
thought to the concept of converting people to my religion.
After all, most everyone whom I associated with—at
church, school, and elsewhere—were Christians. Or at least
if they didn't profess to be Christians, they didn't profess to
be anything else. Now there were people around me who
professed other religions. Wasn't I taught to convert them?
The thought of the task made me shudder.

I had met many wonderful people that first day. There
was a man who I knew was a professed Buddhist. I didn't
know what that meant exactly, except that he did not call
himself a Christian. Could I convert him to my way of thinking or must I ignore him? There were many others in my
class and, though I did not know them well, I knew they
were not necessarily professed Christians. Would I be able
to convert them? Did I even want to try? So many of them—
in fact, most—seemed entirely happy with their way of
understanding. Not with a superficial happiness, but with a
deep internal glow. I felt very fortunate in that respect to be
surrounded by so many people who seemed genuinely
happy. If they weren't Christian, I wondered to myself, and
if I couldn't convert them, how could I ignore such wonderful people? Knowing that we would practice physical

examinations on each other made ignoring them impossible. Far more than the thought of any difficult classes that I might take was the magnitude of the task of converting my classmates to my religion. I slept uneasily that night.

The second day of classes only confirmed my worst fears. I did, indeed, have a lovely bunch of classmates. Most of them seemed genuinely very happy and whole. Worse, of course, was the fact that many of them were happy without being professed Christians. What would I do? What *must* I do with those people, I wondered to myself? In fact, there were some who were of other faiths who seemed far happier and more peaceful than myself. How could I legitimately try to convince them that my way was correct when their way seemed to work so well for them? What if they asked me how an all-loving God could send people to hell? I myself hadn't found an answer to that yet. Fortunately, the reading assignments and studies were enormous from the very beginning, and I could only spend part of my time pondering this question. Still, with physical examination beginning in only the second week of class, I was troubled.

I read in the Bible the words of Jesus who said, "Pray always." (Luke 21:36) I admit that it felt far easier to pray when there was trouble on the horizon. Somehow troubles always seemed to bring me back to my thought of my need for guidance from God. With the great emotional and spiritual trouble that I was feeling, I began to pray. In fact, for nearly that first week of class, I prayed in all of my spare moments. "Lord, please show me what I'm supposed to do," I begged. "Must I really convert these people to my way of thinking, when I don't even feel confident of my way of thinking? Must I really ignore them if they don't think as I do? Please, *please* instruct me in what I should do." After one week of prayer, and a troubled heart and mind, I received an answer. It was in the form of a dream. Though I had never paid much attention to dreams, *this* dream made my answer clear. It was also the first time that I became aware that our dreams are a source of important information and inspiration.

In my dream, I was standing in the living room of my current home. All of my classmates were with me, and we were in a large circle around the room. In fact, we were holding hands in this circle. In the middle of the room was a huge geode that stood nearly three feet tall. A geode, you may know, is a volcanic rock. Inside the rock, a collection of crystals form. In the dream, the geode was cut open and the exposed side was facing me. The classmate to my right said, "What an awesome collection of crystals!" The classmate standing straight across the room from me said, "What crystals? It's a rock." The person standing next to me said, "I guess you could call it a rock, but what a beautiful rock." And the person across from him said, "C'mon, you guys, it's just a rock. Why are you talking like it's something special?" Then it suddenly occurred to us to go around the room and describe what we saw. As we did so, we realized that the scene was different, depending on the angle from which we viewed it. Those on my half of the room saw a crystal garden. Those on the other side of the room saw a plain rock. And those somewhere on the sides could see both and were delighted.

I woke up and a sense of peace flooded over me. Though I had never thought before about interpreting the meaning of my dreams, the answer seemed apparent. We, my classmates and I, were all looking at the same phenomenon— the geode. The only difference in the way it looked to us depended on our perspective. I knew that some of my classmates had studied spiritual traditions that were far older than my own. Those traditions had been given to other cultures and other societies. Could it be that it was the one same Supreme Being with whom we all identified? Yet, depending on the time or the place or the language, we all spoke about it differently? I knew for a fact from my dream, that, for myself, that was the answer. My classmates seemed happy because they *were* happy. They seemed to be spiritual and loving beings because they *were* spiritual and loving beings. The thought that there was another way to be genuinely spiritual without going through a conventional Christian perspective had not occurred to me before. When it did, it felt like light breaking from behind a cloud.

Was this any different from my revelation about the healing arts? Though I recognized many times that technological and allopathic medicine is beneficial, I had also come to recognize and believe that there are many times when another path is really best. Since no one has demonstrated that he or she has the monopoly on healing, it is reasonable to explore all perspectives. What I had already appreciated regarding the healing arts now seemed true regarding "religion" or spirituality. The dream was my answer, though I had not known that dreams could contain answers. I went to class the next day, feeling like a student of the universe instead of just a student of medicine. Now, I wanted to know what those other perspectives were—what they believed and what they said.

How different everything felt to me that next Monday, without the burden of having to convert all of my classmates! Now, I could sit back and be a student of religion as I was of science and medicine. Because I had never fully made the "leap of faith," I still found it hard to believe that I would go to the hot place for eternity just because I was curious. Somehow I believed that God would protect and guide me as I studied other religions outside of my own upbringing.

For the most part, I was quite busy with my studies of anatomy, physiology, biochemistry, histology, cell biology, and philosophy. The classes seemed infinite and infinitely complex. Reading assignments for class were always more than could be accomplished in a single evening. Practical studies included examination of cadavers and palpation and manipulation on classmates. The studies were intense, but exciting. If I had feared that naturopathic medical school was not as "real" as allopathic medical school or somehow less intense, my fears dissolved in the first several weeks of classes. I was studying medicine and science at the same level of intensity that I had always expected I would be.

Lou and I, along with a few other interested students, formed a group of politically active classmates to support and work on behalf of the profession. Most of my time was consumed with classes and my few extracurricular activities.

At other times, when I was taking a break from my studies, I started to read "alternative" scripture. I had a copy of a book called the *Bhagavad Gita*, given to me in an airport once by a bald-headed teen-ager. I never read the book because I was taught that its contents were evil. Still, I could not bring myself to throw it out. With a mock leather cover embossed in gold, it was an imposing document. I had put it on the shelf next to my Bible, but I never dared read it. I had always been taught that to read the scripture of other religions was wrong—a quick ticket to the hot place. Since the time of my dream, realizing that perhaps other religions were simply alternative perspectives on the same Supreme Being, my own outlook was changed. I no longer believed that I would burn for reading someone else's scripture. I was growing to know and love many of my classmates. I also knew that most of them were not of a Christian persuasion. Knowing them and their delightful spirits gave me the courage and curiosity to find out what other religions believed and read. The *Gita* was my first extracurricular reading, and I found it delightful.

The *Bhagavad Gita* is part of the philosophical text of

Hinduism, one of the world's oldest philosophies. The *Gita* is written as an epic poem, a story about a brave warrior and his instruction by The Master. Many of the verses from the *Gita* were reminiscent of what I knew from the Bible. In Sunday school we learned about the Lord Jesus Christ. In the *Gita*, the incarnation of the Lord was called "Krishna." Even the spelling was similar. In the Bible I had learned that God was the "First Cause" of the entire universe. That was the claim of the *Gita* as well. I knew that St. Paul had said, "In him we live, and move, and have our being . . . " (Acts 17:28) In the *Gita* it said that the sun, the moon, the stars, and all creation was situated in him. I felt both amused and delighted by the numerous similarities in various scriptures. They really didn't sound so different from each other at all.

The similarities between medical science and religion were becoming more apparent to me, too. In both religion and medicine, once we think we know the truth, we stop considering other possibilities. Putting ourselves in a box that says "this is the entire truth," we cut ourselves off from other ways of thinking. Just as I had learned as a pre-medical student that my conventional studies were asking me to disavow all knowledge of natural healing, so I recognized that my religious upbringing was asking me to disavow all other philosophical thought. Yet in studying other philosophical thought, I found it to be quite similar to my own. In fact, reading the *Gita* was delightful. Although told in a different way and as a story, the overall message was not different. For so many years I had avoided looking in any other scripture because I had been taught that it was "evil." Now I appreciated that the message was one and the same. The way that the story was told and the language were different. Sometimes understanding something in a different way can be enjoyable and illuminating. What I had thought was quite different, was not. Only my willingness to look

further and consider open-mindedly had shown me this. I
was glad that I had looked.

And then again, in between more of my scientific stud-
ies, I managed to find a second book to read. It was the *Tao
Te Ching*, an important piece of scripture to the Taoists and
Buddhists. It says in the *Tao* that "In the beginning was the
Tao. All things issue from it. All things return again unto it."

"How like the Bible verses I had learned," I mused to myself! "In the beginning was the Word . . . and the Word was
made flesh, and dwelt among us," (John 1:1, 14) I recalled
reading. And "I am the alpha and the omega," (Revelations
22:13) says the Lord, the beginning and the end. A different
language, a different time, but the meaning is the same.
Now I understood a bit more clearly why I had always heard
the Eastern religions say, "All one." As if all of the different
religions could blend together. Why had they not told me
this in Sunday school? The truth: because they themselves
did not know. They had been afraid to look. "What have I
done with my spiritual thought?" I mused to myself. I had
given my own ideas away to what somebody else had told
me without really analyzing or considering the situation
myself. Again, I related that to what I had learned in medicine. We make our minds up, we choose one thing, and we
close our minds to all the other possibilities—even if they
may be complementary. They may be saying a similar thing,
in a slightly different and more usable way. My education of
healing, not just at the level of the physical, but on other
levels as well, felt stronger by the day. I was an enthusiastic
student of science, of philosophy, and of God.

Medical school was as challenging and rewarding as I had
envisioned it would be. It was also as demanding. My original concern that this was not a "real" medical school with
the same level of intensity as conventional medicine had
entirely dissolved. Our courses were rigorous. In addition
to the basic biological sciences and studies of laboratory

medicine and clinical and physical diagnosis, we were required to study natural therapies. Three hours spent in the
laboratory looking through a microscope at slides followed
by another three hours of having our hands on bodies, feeling for the correct alignment of the spine and the normal
placement of the internal organs. Demanding? Yes. I enjoyed it all, and my classmates and instructors as well. For
me, I knew I had chosen the best path. At the end of my first
year of medical school, my belief in the healing power of
nature was tested and settled.

Two weeks after my summer break started at the end of
my first year, I got a call from one of my classmates. He was
a fellow whom I admired very much. Not only a bright student, he was a published author on herbal medicine early
in his career. I liked his energy and his mind. He and his
wife had worked with me on several writing projects. Their
Buddhist perspective was one that I always enjoyed studying. The nature of his call was to offer me a job for several
weeks or perhaps the summer. His diabetic grandfather,
now in his eighties, was being nursed at home with a gan-
grenous foot. He had already lost his big toe and, my friend
explained, was now being told that his foot needed to be
amputated. "Grandpa," as we called him, did not want to
lose his foot. He asked his grandson, "the naturopathic student," to "do some other things" to see if his foot could be
saved. My friend felt that the foot *could* be saved, but that
Grandpa would require round-the-clock care. If I wanted
to, I could earn some extra money working as the night shift
nurse to take care of Grandpa. Not only did the job sound
exciting and the money an enticement, but it was a chance
to see natural therapy in practice. I readily agreed.

The first night I met Grandpa, I saw the extent of his situation. A diabetic for nearly fifty years, he was *still* resistant
to following a good diet. His cooperation level seemed improved, however, by the fact that his left foot was entirely

black. The pain would make him moan and cry in his sleep. There was, however, a detectable pulse still remaining in the foot. On that basis, the naturopathic doctors concurred that his foot might be able to be saved. His conventional physician was angry and divorced himself from the case. With very little in the way of support from the conventional medical community, we began our treatments with Grandpa.

Since I was the night shift nurse, it was my job to apply a charcoal poultice. Charcoal, which has a strong drawing effect, was designed to pull poisons and toxins out of the diseased flesh. In the morning, when I removed the poultice, I would clean the wound and ready him for the day-shift nurse. The student or doctor in charge of the day shift would perform hydrotherapy (hot and cold water treatments) followed by acupuncture and Chinese herbs. Grandpa also received goodly doses of herbal medicine, homeopathic remedies, and a special juice fast. Every night I sat with him, changed his bandage, and then he fell asleep, unless, of course, he needed my help. After about a week, I noticed that he slept soundly through the night.

In four weeks, the color of the foot had changed. Circulation was more obvious; the flesh was closer to a normal color. Grandpa could be up and about with a walker now, moving around under his own steam. We could tell he was recovering because he grew more crotchety by the day. This medical doctor who had disavowed himself of the case weeks before, now re-entered the picture. He agreed to resume the care and watchfulness of the patient and perform any necessary procedures should Grandpa require them. Grandpa, on the other hand, was not highly inspired to see an allopathic doctor. "If you'd have had your way," he shouted angrily one day, "I wouldn't even have a foot now!" Grandpa's sentiments, I knew, were true. If we had not worked so intensively with other therapies, Grandpa would have lost his foot. He probably also would have lost his self-esteem and his life. That's often what happens as a diabetic begins to give up limbs to the disease. There had been little to lose and everything to gain by trying a different way. In this case, the results were successful and dramatic. I got to watch a diseased, so-called "dead limb" restored through natural therapies. This was not thought possible by Grandpa's conventional physicians. But I witnessed. Better yet, I participated. And they even paid me to be a part of that experience! It was a wonderful summer, and it strengthened my dedication to the profession that I was entering.

The second year of medical school was even more exciting and intense than the first. With many of the basic science classes behind, we began studying the practical part of doctoring. Physical diagnosis was one of my favorite classes. How can you look and listen and touch a person and determine what his or her ailment is? That's what we learned in diagnosis class.

We studied laboratory tests and "medical imaging" (the new name given to X-rays, CAT scans, MRIs, and other high-tech ways of looking at the body). Sometimes these tests can be extremely valuable for ruling out certain conditions. One thing that impressed me, however, was the need for the "old- fashioned" information. Most often, a doctor will have a fair idea of what is wrong or what needs to be looked at before any tests are performed. You can't completely diagnose a person simply by taking lots of pictures. As good as our pictures are, there's no one picture that looks at everything. That means that the "old-fashioned" method of diagnosis is also still the "new-fashion" best method of diagnosis. Listening to the patient and what he or she has to tell you is a lost art that is still most valuable. Examining, getting a sense of what is wrong before any tests are ordered. Before tests were available, many of the "old-time" doctors had to be more skillful at diagnosis. There are a lot of modern-day physicians who are quite good as well, but there are some who seem to think you can diagnose a person only by means of laboratory methods. Some of the best ways to detect abnormality have been lost to technology—at least for some. It was fascinating for me to reappreciate the value of basic listening, looking, touching (called palpation), and considering.

We also learned, both in philosophy and science classes, that illnesses have a *cause*. Many times we have been taught to believe that the cause is something outside ourselves. For example, we believe that bacteria and viruses cause disease, and so we aim to kill bacteria and viruses. Yet why, I and others have wanted to know, do some people succumb to bacteria and viruses and not others? Naturopathic philosophy would say that it is the *individual* who either provides a fertile soil for disease or not. Therefore, you can improve the health of individuals and make them more resistant to disease. I believed that, and I had the opportunity to observe that during my studies. Because of my belief that our illnesses and problems have a *cause*, it took me by surprise when I met face to face my own illness.

It happened one day while I was sitting in a public health class. The lecture was a little dry for me that day, but I was actively listening and taking notes nonetheless. Everything in my life seemed fine. I enjoyed school, my chosen work, even this public health class. Suddenly, in the midst of note-taking, I felt a knife being driven through my abdomen. "Save my seat," I said, half jokingly to the classmate sitting next to me. "I'll be back." I didn't come back, however. The last thing I remembered was leaving the class. When I next opened my eyes, I was on a table with bright lights shining on me and eight familiar faces of professors and colleagues looking down at me.

7

POSSIBLY CANCER

"Possibly cancer."

The doctor's words echoed in my head. After my naturopathic physician determined that I had a grapefruit-sized tumor in my abdomen, he recommended that I consult a gynecological surgeon. It was this surgeon who offered me this grave opinion.

For the first few days after my visit with him, my mind and emotions were chaotic. It is difficult to describe the fear that one feels having just received a life-threatening diagnosis. Though I didn't appreciate it at the time, I would later learn to look upon this experience as an invaluable part of my training. In those first few days, however, fear and confusion were all I knew.

Sometimes in the middle of the night I would wake up in a cold sweat. Panic would overtake me at the thought that I had a deadly cancer while still in my early twenties. "What about my parents?" I thought to myself. My mother will be grief stricken—I know how she is. My concern was not only for myself, but for all of those near and dear to me. If no one knew of my illness, if I could keep it to myself, it would be so much easier to bear. How could I tell anyone? How could I break their hearts, I wondered over and over. After several days of being in a state of near shock, I decided it was time to take action. Gathering all my emotional and spiritual resources, I packed my backpack and headed for a nearby wilderness area. A day or two alone in the beauty of nature, I felt sure, would allow me to think and decide—to reason without the background of intense fear that I was experiencing. My decision proved to be a good one.

As I hiked up a strenuous mountain path, feeling weak yet lifted by the beauty, I began to think more clearly. I must overcome this all-embracing fear if I am to make good decisions about my treatment. What was I afraid of, really? I asked myself with earnestness. The answer, I knew, was severalfold. Death, of course, was on the menu. Being in my early twenties, I hadn't spent much time contemplating my own mortality. Suddenly this illness had thrust me face to face with it. Even as I acknowledged my fear, a peaceful remembrance overcame me and I smiled to myself. "Hey, kid," I counseled myself, "you've always been terminal. In this flesh body, you have never for an instant known for certain the day or the hour. If you have cancer and you die from it earlier than you thought, well, the truth is, you were going to die anyway. Who knows, when I come down off this mountaintop and start driving home, I could be hit by a truck and killed instantly—which I also haven't planned on. I have never known the day or the hour and that's the truth," I acknowledged to myself.

"The only difference between now and before was that I have been reminded of my own mortality in this flesh body. That shouldn't be scary. It should've been something that I was always aware of. And if it seems as if my plans or my dreams may be cut shorter than I expect, well, that was always a possibility. In fact, being reminded of my own mortality could actually be a blessing to me, if I make it so. Since none of us knows the day or hour, since none of us knows the length of our lives, shouldn't we always live each day as successfully as we can?" I wondered to myself.

In spite of my fears of the last few days, life was somehow also enlivened for me. I noticed that if I felt love toward someone, it was easier to say it. After all, how much longer did I have, I wondered, to say those words of love that I truly meant? Perhaps there was a lesson in this after all. A lesson that can only be gained by remembering that none of us ever knows the day or hour. We work, we plan, we put happiness off "in the future." We wait for some magic day when we have more money, more time, less stress, less responsibilities, a mobile home. Suddenly I realized that the only life I have is in this very moment. If I have tomorrow or next week or next year, it is a gift. A gift that I have never known whether or not I would see. My illness hasn't changed that—it has helped me see what a gift the *now moment* is. I was grateful for the revelation. I could feel the fear dissolving.

Another thought gave me further consolation: I am a divine, eternal being, not just a mere mortal, I reminded myself. It is science, not religion, but science that says that energy cannot be created or destroyed by ordinary means. There is an energy that is present in our bodies when we are alive. At death it is gone. But science says that it does not cease to be. Every religion talks about that "energy" that we are—the soul. Every religion and philosophy that I have studied believes in it, knows about it. Even science, which says that it divorces itself from religion, acknowledges that we must be eternal. I didn't need to be convinced from science. I knew from somewhere deep inside myself that the fact of my continuance beyond the body was assured. But had I looked for confirmation, I would have found it—and from any direction I looked. "Surely," I said aloud to myself, "I am a divine, eternal being. My life, and who I am as a soul, transcends the body. My life and who I am as a soul outlives the body. Therefore, the death of my flesh would only be a transition for my soul. I know this, and I know it with certainty. There had simply been nothing in my life to cause me to contemplate it deeply. Now there is." And out of the midst of fear came an incredible feeling of warmth. The fear was further dissolving in my remembrance.

There was one other fear I acknowledged to myself. Not the fear of death, for I have always known that I would die someday. Not the fear that death would be the end of me, for I now knew that I was a divine, eternal being. Perhaps the greatest fear was that of suffering. Cancer, like some other life-threatening illnesses, can drag on for days, weeks, months, and even years. And not only would the pain be great for me, but for my family and loved ones that would be called on to care for me. That, I decided, was a far bigger fear even than death. How could I face that fear squarely, I wondered to myself? Was there a consolation? The warm feeling that had begun to come over me sustained me. The beauty of nature sustained me. I would continue to walk and work and ask until I found the answer.

"Almighty God, Lord Jesus Christ, saints, guardian angels, whoever is out there to help me," I prayed aloud, "help me find the answer to this question." No sooner had I said the words, than other words and pictures flashed across the screen of my mind. I recalled the verse from the Bible which said, "Suffering lasts but for a night, and joy cometh in the morning." (Psalm 30:5) Compared to the fact of my ongoing nature, my eternalness, even a whole lifetime, was brief.

"There are many ways to face pain," I reminded myself. I already knew from my previous personal experience with pain that a deeply meditative state was very helpful. Of course, there are pain medications, if pain ever becomes extremely severe, that can be used. "Attitude is all-important," I told myself. Those who said, "I am weak, I have a low threshold for pain," would find it to be so. Those who believed they were strong and had a high threshold for pain would also find it to be so. I was lucky. I considered myself to be strong. Whatever comes, I can face it, I told myself. After all, life doesn't happen to us at random. There is a reason, a cause for my illness, and there are answers that will either cure me or allow me to do what I need to do to live through this disease. "One day at a time," I heard the words from the twelve-step program. I don't have to solve the problem of tomorrow or worry about what would happen next month or next year. I have only to concern myself with this day, this moment. I can face whatever life brings me. When death comes from whatever cause, I want to be ready. And they can write on my tombstone as I have seen quoted elsewhere, "She lived until she died." Yes, I decided with a surge of strength that rocked my being, I will live fully and wholly until I die. I will work with my illness in whatever way I find, but I will not put off the joy of living until I am "cured." None of us ever knows when death will come. Living is for today, for this moment. As I finished the thought, I rounded the curve on the mountain trail and came to a beautiful vista. Standing high atop the mountain, gazing out onto a forest valley, I almost felt as if I could fly. "This suffering has brought me to new heights of strength," I thought to myself. "If I can't get my 'goodies' from this trouble, then what's it worth?" I smiled at the thought. Ah, what stories I'll be able to share with my patients. My smile grew even wider, and I felt a catch of joy in my throat. Joy . . . and rejoicing . . . where only an hour before there had been terror.

I returned home from the mountain exultant. Fear had been replaced by a tremendous desire to learn, to be, and to heal. With all the vigor of a military strategist, I evaluated my circumstance and diagnosis. I determined that if, indeed, my diagnosis was cancer, a mass this large was already a near-death sentence. In other words, if it was cancer and it was that big, surgery wouldn't buy me much time.

On the other hand, if this were simply a large, benign fluid-filled cyst, then except for the possibility of peritonitis and pain, I could take time to explore whatever treatment I chose. The risk of surgery and general anesthesia, I calculated, was probably no less than the risk of another infection from the cyst.

How much could be accomplished through good nutrition, exercise, homeopathy, and all the natural treatments I was studying? It might be a long time as a medical student before I would find a patient willing to diligently try natural treatments in his or her own behalf in such a case. "I could be my own science lab," I recognized enthusiastically. "I can devise my own natural treatment plan and follow it myself. That will give me the opportunity to witness, yet again, whether or not this kind of therapy really works. I get to be my own physician and test my own therapies. No one can take that away from me." And that's exactly what I decided to do.

My naturopathic physician felt that my logic was sound and supported my decision. When I then returned to my gynecologist surgeon and announced my decision, I received a different reaction: he was angry. "Don't you realize that we must do surgery right away?" he scolded me harshly. "Who's this 'we'?" I snapped back at him.

"This is my body. I'm well informed on the pros and cons of this. Look me straight in the eyes and tell me that if this is cancer, your surgery is going to buy me a whole bunch of time," I demanded. He stared back but was silent. "And if it's

benign, I want to find out what I can do through other methods."

He shook his head. "You naturopathic types are all alike,"
was his retort. "Well, do what you have to do."

"Thank you, doctor," I said earnestly. "If I need surgery, I
still want you to be my doctor. I just have to try it another
way first. Any of us would try the medicine we most believe
in first, wouldn't we?" I was pleading for understanding.

"I suppose so," he acknowledged reluctantly.

I did not function alone to devise my own treatment plan.
I consulted two naturopathic doctors, had the necessary
evaluations, and took their advice into account. My strategy included a very specific diet, hydrotherapy, herbal and
homeopathic programs. In addition, I was using daily castor oil packs from the Cayce readings, as well as Atomidine
and meditation. Things seemed to be working for several
months, and I felt just fine. I was back in school and doing
better than ever academically. In a way, it was another type
of blessing. Before this, I had not been paying good attention to my personal routine—my diet and exercise. With the
illness providing strong motivation, I was faithful to my
plan.

I would go for walks and pray for understanding. "Lord, I
believe that I have allowed or even created this illness for a
reason. If it's a lesson that I have chosen to learn, please help
me know what that lesson is, please help me find it so that I
can embrace the truth that this contains." One day toward
the very end of the term, several months into my personal
healing program, the symptoms struck again. Sudden, severe onslaught of intense pain. This time when I passed out,
I hit my head hard on the door frame. Now I had a lump the
size of an egg on my head in addition to the peritonitis. I
was still determined to continue. A week later, nearly fully
recovered from my bout of sudden pain and infection, a
second episode of pain struck. I had not been well enough

to go back to school, and it appeared that I would miss even more time. Now I was frightened, but for a different reason. Final examinations for the semester were scheduled the following week. Realizing how sick I was, I knew that I would not be able to take them. The illness was starting to interfere with my studies. Was there something else I needed to be doing? I got on the telephone and made a lot of calls.

I talked to doctors all over the country. Of course, the allopathic recommendations were the same: anything that big needs to be surgically removed. The follow-up recommendations varied somewhat. There were different types of hormone-suppressing therapies that could be used. Since follow-up treatment seemed like the smallest part of the consideration to me, I paid little attention.

Some of the naturopathic doctors recommended things that I was already doing. Finally, I called Dr. B., one of the oldest and most respected physicians in the naturopathic profession. He listened thoughtfully as I described my circumstance, and then he said, "I think you'd better have surgery."

My heart fell. I was hoping for words of sage wisdom and advice, and felt let down. "But why?" I pleaded to know.

"Well," he began, "something the size of a grapefruit is pretty large. The body does have the ability to reabsorb tumors and masses, of course, but by the time something gets that big, you're really asking the body to do a very big job. Since this keeps interfering with your life and your school work, wouldn't it be easier to simply have it surgically removed?" he questioned. "Then you can continue all of your natural therapies. Strengthen your body, enhance your immune system, balance your hormones, and ask your body to finish up the 'details' of the healing. That will also prevent you from having a recurrence.

"Dana," he said, as if to get my attention more completely, "you are obligated to think holistically because of your chosen path. Don't deny any reasonable form of treatment, even if it's outside of what you personally practice as a physician. Healing can come from any direction. Surgery, when it's necessary, is a very helpful treatment. It's also a very old treatment. Think about it. You've got to make your own decisions. You asked for my advice, and I'm offering it. Something that big that keeps causing you problems—I think it needs to come out with a knife."

His words were "to the point," but his voice was kind. "Thank you, Dr. B.," I said hesitantly.

"Let me know what you decide. I'll be praying for you."

I lay in bed and thought about it. The peritonitis this time was so painful that it caused my breathing to be very shallow. I looked with dread on having to get out of bed to go to the bathroom. Though finals were next week, I felt far too sick to study. It was an effort to even open my eyes, much less to hold a book. Perhaps Dr. B. was right.

There was nothing much to do but lie in bed and try to sleep or meditate. Perhaps it was out of my meditations or my dream state that I finally made my decision. Dr. B. was right. Something this big could be surgically removed and followed up with natural methods. Then, too, I caught myself wondering whether I was harboring a "them versus us" attitude. "Who cares about that? I'm looking for what will make me better. I'm in such pain now that I can't move, and it looks as if I'll miss taking my final examinations at school. If I have this thing, whatever it is, surgically taken out, my body will have less repair work to do. I can use my natural therapies for follow-up (instead of drugs). Now with a different attitude, I had a friend take me to the hospital.

Being a patient, not just in the doctor's office, but in a hospital, was another invaluable experience. I had always been on the other side of the situation. Now, *I* was the one lying in bed.

I was in my bed for six hours before anyone came to me. When a nurse finally appeared, she said she was there to catheterize me. She inserted a tube and began to leave the room. "Wait a minute," I said. "I thought you were going to put a tube in my bladder?"

"I did."

"No, you didn't."

"What do you think I just did?" she questioned.

"You put the tube in my vagina, not in my urethra," I said slowly and distinctly.

She seemed surprised that I knew the anatomical terms for my body parts. "And how do you know that?" she countered.

"Well," I said, "this is my body. I've been living in it for quite a few years now, and I know my holes."

She glared at me. "You've been catheterized—correctly," she snapped and turned and left the room.

I could've been angry, but it was too funny. A while later I stumbled out of bed go to the bathroom. Since I had not been catheterized, it was still a necessity for me to find a toilet in which to urinate. The nurse from the next shift entered the room while I was washing my hands.

"What are you doing out of bed?" she asked.

"Oh, I had to go to the bathroom," I told her.

"You've been catheterized already," she reminded me.

"No, not really," I said and climbed back into bed. I had left the tube in place—the wrong place, to show that I wasn't crazy.

She examined me and said with a laugh, "Who did this to you?"

"Oh, the nurse on the shift before you," I said.

"Well, we're going to have to find out where she learned her anatomy," she grinned, and we smiled at each other. "Now, I'm really going to catheterize you," she told me, and did.

An hour later, a different nurse entered with a clipboard in her hand. "This is your release and consent form for surgery," she told me. "Please read it and sign on these four lines," she pointed them out. I read the form while she stood by my bedside and waited. At one point it said that they were going to remove my left ovary.

"Excuse me, nurse," I pointed to the document. "This form has a mistake in it. It's my right ovary that needs the surgery. And I really don't want the whole ovary removed—just the cyst taken off."

"No, it's your left ovary," she contradicted.

"No, it isn't," I replied. "I've seen my ultrasound, number one, but secondly, I know which side the pain is on. I'm not signing this. There's been a mistake made. Please correct this." She took the clipboard out of my hand and exited the room. I was glad that I had chosen a church-related hospital, I thought to myself. What would it be like to be in a for-profit institution? I would have smiled except the situation seemed a little extreme.

A few minutes later the surgeon himself entered. He shook his head in that characteristic way and sat in a chair beside my bed. "Dana," he said, "we want to remove the whole ovary, not just the cyst. And if it looks suspicious for cancer, we'll take out both ovaries; in fact, we'll do a complete hysterectomy."

I stared at him quizzically. "That's not what I understood, doctor. This is what I thought you and I had agreed on," I said, and I began to remind him of our previous discussion. "Once inside, you will remove just the cyst from my ovary. Unless, of course, it appears to you to be cancerous, in which case you will remove the entire ovary. Then I would like you to simply look at the opposite ovary. If it appears to be disease-free, leave it in place. I understand the high risk of having ovarian cancer travel from one ovary to another. I also understand all the problems I will have if it later turns out not to be cancer and in my twenties I go through meno-pause. Anything that looks diseased, please remove. I trust your judgment on this, but you do not have my permission to take out parts that appear well. I do not want a complete hysterectomy unless everything in there appears to be highly diseased." My voice was steady and certain. I knew what I wanted and expected. I had done my homework. This man, skillful as he was, was still my employee. I knew that. He knew that I knew that.

"All right," he said. "I believe that you are well informed in this decision. The nurse will be back in with a new consent form. I'll see you in surgery." There was little warmth in his voice as he turned and left the room.

Immediately after his exit, the nurse returned with her clipboard. Without a word she handed it back to me. The form had been changed. It now asked me to give my con-sent to have my right ovary resected, which means the "tumor only" removed. "Oh, it was the right," I said, as if surprised. "Umm," she grunted without true acknowledg-ment.

When she left the room, I lay in my bed in complete won-derment. "What would a patient, who was shy or unknowl-edgeable, do in a situation like this?" I wondered. I know enough about medicine and anatomy to speak up for my-self, but most people don't. It's not necessarily that this place is so inept. Ineptness occurs in all areas in all types of medi-cine, no doubt. So does great skill. But these mistakes are enough to be almost laughable. I did laugh, for my own cir-cumstance, but feared for other patients.

Finally, a quiet and very friendly little man entered my room. Ken, as he introduced himself, was Korean. He was going to give me a pre-operative injection before I was taken to surgery. This would help me feel more calm and relaxed as they prepared me. His injection was the best I'd ever had—I scarcely felt it. A couple of minutes later, however, I became very nauseous and began to retch. A second injection was administered, this time something to counter the nausea. It helped only a little, and I felt quite sick to my stomach as they wheeled me to the surgical suite.

I was taken down the hall and put in a dimly lit room by myself. "Pre-op," they told me. I would be here for a few minutes while the medication continued to take effect. I could feel myself losing touch with my consciousness. I began to pray, "Lord, let the work of the surgeon, the anesthesiologist, and all concerned be blessed. Let Thy will be done. Let the good thing happen." I believed then, and still do, that the anesthesia is far more of a threat than the actual surgery. When a man leaned over my bed and introduced himself as Dr. George, my anesthesiologist, I felt relieved. Now I had the chance to say a blessing with the man who would put me to sleep. "Nice to meet you," I said, through my half-hazed consciousness. "I appreciate the work you do and may God bless your work on me this day." Dr. George looked at me and laughed.

"Well," he said with more than a hint of arrogance, "I've done this procedure hundreds of times." What does that mean, I wondered to myself? That he doesn't need the help of a Higher Power because he's so skillful? Suddenly I was nervous. I squeezed my eyes shut tightly and began to pray again. "Lord, please, please," I pleaded, "what is with this anesthesiologist that he doesn't know that he needs You to do his work?" I thought inside my head. In what seemed like only an instant later, I heard another voice. A different face leaned over my bed, and I heard a voice saying, "Hello, Dana. I'm Dr. Saunder. I'm afraid that Dr. George was called away suddenly on another case. I'm going to be your anesthesiologist instead."

"Oh," I said, somewhat surprised that my prayer had actually been answered. "Nice to meet you, and may God bless your work."

"Oh, yes, thank you," he said sincerely. "I would never want to go into that operating room without the blessing of the Almighty. I know that it's not me, but He, who does the work."

Though I couldn't move my body, a part of me felt as if it were jumping for joy. "Yes, thank You, thank You, Lord, thank You." I may have said it aloud as I thought it. Now I was ready for surgery. The man who would "put me under" knew about God. The next I remember I was back in my room at the hospital.

"The worst case of endometriosis I've ever seen," the surgeon said, shaking his head as he entered the room. "I took off a huge cyst from your ovary—it wasn't cancer. The other ovary looked fine, I left it alone. You had so much endometrial tissue on all of your internal organs . . . well, I've never seen a case like that before. Your appendix was covered. I did have to take that out. You must have been having a lot of pain with every menstrual cycle. Lord, I don't even know how you were up and walking around. Anyway, things went well; you should be out in four days."

"Thanks, doc," I said and was truly grateful. Then I reminded him, "Uh, I don't have any health insurance, remember? I'll be paying you, the other doctors, and the hospital back as soon as I can, but it will take some time." I was discharged the following morning.

That first night after surgery I was sleeping peacefully when the nurse entered my room and awakened me. "I'm here to give you an injection of pain medication," she announced.

"Well, really, I'd prefer not to," I told her. "I seem to be sleeping O.K., and if I don't move a lot, it doesn't hurt too much. I'd really rather pass on this. I think I'll recover more quickly without it."

"Well," she said, "my orders are to give it to you. I can't change that."

"Well, please go ask whoever you need to," my voice was only half sincere. In my half-asleep, half-awake state I did not really want to argue with the nurse. Without responding one way or the other, she rolled me on my side. All of a sudden, I felt a searing pain in my left hip. As I turned to look, I saw that she had not one, but two huge syringes that she had thrust into my flesh. The pain of the injection was far worse than any other pain I was currently experiencing. The next morning, at the time of my discharge, I saw that my entire left buttock was black and blue. That bruise remained for nearly two months.

Once at home, I expected to recover quickly. The surgery had been successful; the tumor was removed. On an additional happy note, there was no cancer found and I still had all of my female organs, including ovaries. Now I could go back to school and get back about my healing work and all would be well. For two days I seemed to improve steadily. Then something happened. I began running a high fever and having a lot of pelvic pain again. The surgeon examined me and told me that I had a post-surgical infection. "Don't even ask me about using herbs," he said. "This is a serious infection and will require strong antibiotics." Before I could even ask questions, he went on. "This is a type of bacteria that was introduced during the surgery, and it's deep in a place where it doesn't usually have access. I'm beginning to believe that all of these natural therapies that you use can be helpful and effective," he admitted, "but this is an unnatural situation. You need a synthetic antibiotic," he emphasized. I did not argue. After all, though I didn't tell him, many antibiotics are "natural substances." Tetracycline, penicillin, ampicillin . . . these are all naturally derived from mold. As a naturopath, I was being trained to understand, use, and prescribe antibiotics. I really didn't have a philosophical problem with taking one. I was too sick to point this out to him and submitted willingly. A few days after beginning the antibiotic, my symptoms began to clear, and it was apparent that I genuinely was on my way to recovery.

Though I suppose I sprang back fairly quickly, it seemed like a much longer process than I had anticipated. The year was well into summer now. I had missed all of my final exams, and so I had to study and take make-up tests. It was nearly three months before I felt genuinely well again. During my recovery period, I was still on a special diet, doing herbs, homeopathic remedies, hydrotherapy, daily meditation, regular castor oil packs, prayer, and more. I made getting well a nearly full-time job. In addition to my natural therapies, I was also on the hormone therapy that the surgeon had recommended. I was doing what I thought was the best of both conventional and naturopathic worlds. I fully expected to recover. I didn't. Toward the end of summer, that characteristic sudden onset pain occurred again. This time I pushed deep inside my own abdomen and a chill went through me. I could feel it. The cyst was back.

I went immediately to the surgeon for evaluation. He performed an ultrasound test and confirmed my own diagnosis. "It appears that the cyst has returned," he told me. It had not even been three months since my surgery, and I pointed that out to him. "How could this be?" I demanded to know. "Wasn't hormone therapy supposed to suppress the regrowth of this thing?"

"Well, yes, it was supposed to do that," he said. "But apparently it hasn't. Your therapies haven't worked either." His words seared deep into my soul. "It looks like we'll have to go back in and do more surgery," he announced and stood to leave the room.

"Wait a minute, doctor," I said in a demanding tone, and he turned on his heel again to look at me. "Does this look like a dumb face?" I asked, pointing to my own face. "You said my treatment didn't work, and apparently you're right."

I was agitated. "But you cut the thing out and that didn't work either," I said to him half shouting. "Why would I go through that again if it doesn't work?" I demanded to know. He had no answer.

"Give me a call when you've decided," he said as if he hadn't heard my words. He turned and left the room.

I went home to rethink the situation. My natural therapies by themselves had not worked. I trusted all of my naturopathic doctors—they were some of the best. I trusted myself and knew that I had been diligent with my treatments. The problem was still there. Next, I had consulted the best of what conventional medicine had to offer. I had submitted to both the surgery and the hormone therapy for follow-up. Still, the condition persisted. Clearly, neither one of these two disciplines had the whole answer here. In fact, I wasn't sure that either discipline had any answer. "Now what would I do?" I wondered. There was no fear this time. "Why do I keep creating or allowing this big thing to grow inside my body?" Then I watched for dreams or intuition and nothing came. "There's got to be an explanation for this. There's an answer here somewhere. A reason. Just doing the correct physical treatments is not enough. If I don't find the answer as to why this is here, it will not go away. I must keep looking, and keep looking in other places.

"Perhaps the answer is somewhere deep in mind or soul. After all, hadn't Edgar Cayce searched high and low for a cure for his condition? When none could be found, he finally consulted his own interior wisdom and then the answer came. Perhaps I could do that with myself," I wondered. "What have I got to lose? Everything else that has seemed reasonable, I have tried. Even a few things that I was philosophically against, I have tried. The condition's here, I must keep looking." Now my thoughts were turned more toward the mental and spiritual aspects of my illness rather than just the physical alone. I maintained what I believed to be the best diet and exercise program and other treatments. But I knew that my search for an answer must continue.

I knew that one of my professors at school did a treatment called neurolinguistic programming (NLP). It is very similar to hypnosis. I decided to go to him and ask him to "put me under"—the highly relaxed state. I told him that I wanted him to hypnotize me and then ask me if I knew what was wrong with me. Though he said he had never done that before, he was willing.

The first session I spent with him I have no recollection of. I later heard what I said, however, because he made a cassette tape. On the tape I heard my own voice. I was saying, "This is Dana, the higher self of Dana." The voice—my voice—said that I had given this illness permission to be in my body as a learning experience. I went on to say that I needed to learn important lessons about healing that I would not be taught in school. The only way for me to acquire these lessons was to create my own opportunity to learn them. When I heard the tape played back, I was mystified. "What lessons?" I wanted to know. Why would I say this to myself?

I returned for a second session. This time, I told him, "Please tell me that I will remember what I say. I want to hear it myself while I'm saying it—not just on a tape. Do you think we can do that?"

"I don't know," he said. "I didn't know we could do what we did last time either. We'll give it a try."

He put me in a deeply relaxed state. Then I heard him ask a question. First, he asked to speak to my subconscious mind. Suddenly, I heard a voice. "This is the higher self of Dana Myatt," I heard the voice say. I was surprised. It was my voice and suddenly I realized that my lips were moving. But the voice did not seem to be coming from the control of my conscious mind. In fact, it seemed to be my conscious mind that was listening and some other part of me that was doing the speaking. I was fascinated as the voice continued. "There are lessons to be learned about healing that are not being taught in any medical school," I heard myself emphasize. "Lessons about who we really are, in a spiritual sense. Lessons about the great power that thought has over the physical body. There are other lessons of compassion and understanding that can't be gotten in a classroom. How would you ever know what it feels like to be a patient in a hospital unless you had been there? Does anyone really understand what it feels like to carry the diagnosis of a life-threatening illness?" my voice questioned me. "Can anyone know the fear that comes with uncertainty? I don't think so," I heard my voice say. "You had lessons to learn, my dear," I went on. "You chose to learn them quickly, just as if you had taken another year of medical school. For you, your illness was another year of medical school. And now that you have learned and experienced these things, you are free to chose to move on."

My own voice then went on to describe what would be helpful in my healing process. I told myself that I needed to continue my current physical treatments and develop my new-found understanding of compassion and correct attitude through personal prayer and meditation. I also told myself that I would need no further sessions of this kind.

I thanked the doctor who had helped me with the NLP, took my second cassette tape, and left. I never went back. I guess I never felt a need to. I did as I had instructed myself, and my condition healed within two months. The large re-grown cyst spontaneously disappeared. My surgeon was mystified.

"Well, maybe there's something to those natural therapies after all," he conceded when he reexamined me. "There's no evidence of a cyst on ultrasound at this time."

I wanted to claim a total victory for my herbs and diet,

but in truth I couldn't. "Yes, that was part of it," I confessed, "but there was more. There was an emotional and spiritual component that I had no idea about. If I hadn't found that, I don't think the other treatments would have worked."

He shook his head and cracked a smile for the first time that I could remember. "Well, good luck to you, Dana. Good luck." He shook my hand and left the room.

There was still more learning to be had from this experience. Bills began pouring in from the hospital, from the surgeon, from the anesthesiologist, from the nurses. Every day that I went to the mailbox, it seemed there was another bill. "Why can't they all put their bills together and just send me one bill?" I complained to a friend. "I think I have a bill for $83.00 from the fellow who emptied the garbage can in my room," I said half in fun, full in earnest. When the bills stopped arriving, I totaled them up. Just over $7,000.00 was what my two days in the hospital had cost me. The total was identical to a year of medical school tuition.

I recalled my voice from the NLP session, "You've created an extra year of school for yourself." Indeed I had. And because I had no health insurance, I had to take the rest of that year off and work part-time to earn the money to pay back my medical debt. It was an extra year of learning. I would not have wanted to miss a single heartbeat of that experience.

8

LITTLE BIRD FLIES

It was with excitement and some hesitation that I began my third year of medical school. I was eager to resume my studies, to begin seeing patients in clinic. It was during the third year that we would start to become "real" doctors, working more with actual people in addition to the book learning. I had some degree of trepidation, however, about starting my third year, because all my classmates were strangers. Oh, I knew them by name, of course, but they were not the students that I had started class with. All of my buddies were now a year ahead of me in school. I would be joining a class that had already bonded, already formed its social groups and study groups. I was the outsider, the newcomer to the class. It felt somewhat uncomfortable, odd. The experience gave me a new appreciation of how people feel when they move to a new town or a new school or a new place. With this, as with all things since my illness, I found new depths of opportunity, however. If my illness had taught me anything, it had taught me this: look for the good and the learning in every circumstance. What had I learned from my time of physical challenge? I had learned to face the fear of pain, suffering, and death, and emerge victorious. I had learned to put my own system of medicine and another system of medicine to the test and found them both wanting. I had the opportunity to learn that mind and emotions are also a part of many of our physical ailments in a way that I might never have learned in the classroom. And, I had had the opportunity to learn that every problem is an opportunity. It was, I thought to myself, as Edgar Cayce had said, that problems may become either stumbling blocks or stepping-stones. Since the time of my own physical challenge, I had begun to view all my problems as opportunities for growth, especially soul growth. And so, being in this classroom and having to make new friendships and new associations and new study partners, I accepted all this with some degree of trepidation, but also as an opportunity. After all, what other good choice was there?

It was interesting to note what was important to me for my own illness experience and what was important to others. Most people wanted to know about the illness. What was wrong? How it felt. Wasn't I scared? What I most wanted to tell them—and did—was what I learned from the experience. It was, I explained, an opportunity to remember myself as a spiritual being. To "get real" about the fact that I only have the present moment that I live in . . . always . . . ever. It was a reminder that each moment of life is to be embraced, not a magic "someday" down the road which may never come. It was a chance to see that in the midst of the blackest moment, there is learning and goodness and growth to be had. Somehow, it seemed that most people didn't want to hear all that. The experiences with pain, the suffering, and the fear were what people were asking me to talk about. When I lost interest in those conversations, they lost interest in asking. And so, to my relief, it was very soon before no one really questioned me about the time I had lost from school. I was not called on again—very often at least—to relate the experience, and it faded from my mind. (It faded so completely, in fact, that when I wrote this book in its entirety, I forgot to tell this tale. Many years later, as I was completing the patient stories for this book, I attended a conference of doctors, a weeklong retreat high in the mountains. Everyone knew that I was working on a book because I would sneak away at breaks to put in time with the chapters. One day at lunch someone asked me if I had any personal knowledge of the condition of endometriosis. "Oh, yes," I remarked. "I have a lot of personal experience with that. I spent an entire year recovering from a serious case of it myself. In fact, it was my 'extra year' of medical school." Someone else at the table remarked, "Well, you are telling about that in your book, aren't you?" At that moment, I realized I had forgotten to tell the tale. Why? Because per-haps—I believe it so—I have entirely healed from the experience. I keep the learning and the growth within my heart and soul. It is part of what I do, what my life is now, and the exciting tales you will read in Part Two of this book. But the hurt, the pain—I have completely forgotten those. They are nothing to me now except the good that I have kept. It was not until someone reminded me of this event that I even thought to include it in this book. "But don't you think that would be important for others to know that you have had a personal experience with illness?" I was asked. "Of course. And now that you've mentioned it, I'm amused that I did not recall the experience." And now I add this again into my diary. It is indeed part of my life story. The part that I have retained is the wonderful learning that this experience allowed me to have. Somehow, it seems, I have discarded all the rest. I can retell, and with enthusiasm, if it is brought back to my conscious remembrance.)

Third year of medical school was very exciting for me. As it turned out, there was one member of my class who never had really "settled in," never found a good study-buddy to work with. Luckily for me, as well as he, we found that we were a good complement to each other when it came to studying naturopathic medicine. We each had our areas of strength and weakness—a good complement for study partners. I managed to get him through cardiology, and he pulled me through homeopathy. Together, we studied, learned, passed all of our examinations, and became doctors together. Every now and then my old study-buddy, Louise, would call me.

"Dana, where are you when I need you?" she would lament to me on the telephone. "I'm studying (whatever it was she was studying)," she would tell me. "Oh, I'm studying with Jane and Andrea and they're good, but it's just not like you and me."

"Well, sorry, Lou," I'd tell her. "I miss you, too. The Lord giveth and the Lord taketh away," I'd tell her and then we'd laugh together. I'm sure we both did fine without each other's company for study, but somehow it felt good to think that we still needed each other.

My third year of studies was one of the most exciting ever! This was the year that we started seeing patients. Though always working with a fourth-year student and a doctor, we got to observe and have some input into every case. Sometimes our observations were important to solving the mysteries of the case. Most times we simply stumbled over our inadequacies, but we learned from them. There were times when my perceptions, especially of the Cayce readings and my own experiences gained from my illness, were not appreciated. I tried to chalk that frustration up to yet another learning experience.

I remember one day when a woman came into the teaching clinic with some kind of a physical complaint. As a learning experience, I was sent by myself into the room to interview the patient. Though her symptoms were that of rheumatoid arthritis, what she in essence told me was that her problem was a moral dilemma. It seemed that she was a fundamentalist Christian. Her husband had committed an act of adultery some twenty-three years ago and she had never forgiven him. She didn't tell me the story quite that succinctly, but that in essence is what she told me. The symptoms of her illness had started shortly after she found out about the affair. Over the years the symptoms had progressed until now they were quite severe. She had tried a number of different treatments and remedies and was still sick. "What did we have to offer?" she wanted to know. The answer seemed so clear to me, as if the woman were wearing a billboard into the clinic. All of the physical remedies that she had tried had been to no avail. And why? I reflected back upon my own case. Clearly, she was telling me that there was an area of thought or emotion that had not been resolved. I was absolutely confident as I spoke with her that the "center of gravity" of the difficulty revolved around this incident. Because she had been willing to tell me about her religious faith, I spoke to her in "her own language." Cayce often said that we must meet each person at his or her own level of consciousness. I believed then and still do that this is good advice. Now that I understood a variety of religions and religious perspectives, I was more fluent in meeting people at their level of understanding. It seemed very clear to me why I had been the one who had been sent to talk to this woman.

Her invisible, but obvious to me, billboard read: "I'm having a crisis in my spiritual life that is contributing to my physical illness." The woman's words, her description of herself, all pointed in that direction. Because she brought the topic up, I encouraged more conversation. I pointed out to her that old held resentments could affect the physical body. If she had never forgiven her husband, that could be causing her distress. She agreed and seemed eager to converse. We talked about forgiveness, how it was a part of her religion, how her failure to forgive completely and fully thus far may have been irritating her at the very core of her spiritual belief. She grew animated, wanting to know more about forgiveness. My time was up with the patient, and I was supposed to report to my professor. I left the room to tell her what I had found.

"What's wrong with her on a physical level?" the professor demanded.

"I'm telling you," I emphasized back, "her physical problem probably has roots in this spiritual dilemma. She's tried everything we would think to try. She's had conventional drugs. She's had acupuncture and herbs and diet changes. And she's still stuck in this illness. She practically came in here wearing a sign that said: 'I have a spiritual/moral dilemma, and I want to talk about it.' When I started to speak of it with her, she came alive again. She needs to be counseled at her level of spiritual understanding. A long-held resentment relative to her husband is, in my opinion, the seat of her illness." Just like in second grade. Just like with my surgeon. The professor and I now stared at each other, longly, deliberately.

"Dana," another professor jumped from his chair in the conference room and joined our group, "we want to know what is physically wrong with her. It's really not our place to talk to people about their religious beliefs," he said. My mouth fell open.

"What do you mean?" I was incredulous. "I am being trained to treat people at every level of imbalance, right?" I challenged back. "In homeopathy, we learn to identify the 'center of gravity' of the case. Is this problem primarily spiritual, mental, or physical? The woman's problem manifests on the physical, but its roots are in the spiritual," I explained to him, as if I needed to. "She's already tried a lot of therapies on the physical level. If I simply give her another physical treatment without looking for other, higher levels of cause, then I might as well be in allopathic medical school." The room was silent at my words.

My head was spinning. I had been elated to discover what appeared to be the real problem in a patient, and now my professors were telling me I shouldn't have even broached the subject with her. Here we were again talking about physical level causes of physical illness. And perhaps, I thought to myself, you can dabble with the body-mind connection, but please don't talk about a person's religious beliefs. It's too inflammatory a subject. My fears were confirmed when the professor spoke again.

"Dana," the professor explained to me, trying to calm himself, "the medicine that we practice is scientific, even though many folks don't know that yet. If we go 'too far off' talking about 'far-out things,' people won't understand that the use of herbs and good nutrition and exercise and positive thought is scientific. We're trying to bring credibility to our profession. You might make somebody angry if you bring up the subject of religion."

"Yes," I acknowledged eagerly, "I might make somebody angry if that's not that person's level of consciousness. This woman came in practically wearing a billboard that said, 'I need to talk about this moral dilemma.' It was so easy to get this information out of her. The onset of her illness began with this moral dilemma and has grown worse over the years as her resentment has grown. I didn't offend her by asking these questions. She seemed relieved to finally find someone who would talk about this." Our voices were higher now, and we spoke in a more frenzied pitch.

The other professor interrupted our heated discussion. "Dana, we are trying to conduct a specific protocol using herbs, homeopathy, castor oil packs, and diet. It was your job to determine which of these treatments the patient needs, and in what sequence or series. We will have no more discussion about this patient's religion or her 'moral dilemma.' You have fifteen minutes to work up a treatment protocol and present it to me for this patient. In the meantime, I will go interview the patient. Do you think you will be able to do this?" The female professor's eyes were piercing.

"Yes," I said flatly, trying not to feel anger.

I worked up a treatment plan. I suggested the herbs, the homeopathic remedy, the alkaline diet, and the four consecutive days of castor oil packs that the patient would need to recuperate. What my professors didn't know, but I did, was that all of our naturopathic treatments were also Edgar Cayce treatments. Because I had been studying the Cayce readings for so long, knowing how to use castor oil packs and the alkaline diet came easy for me. I was finished before my fifteen-minute time allotment.

The professors re-entered the conference room and looked at my treatment program. "Why four consecutive days of castor oil packs?" one professor wanted to know. The other professor interrupted before I could answer. "I think it would be easier for her to use three packs a week, every other day." They began to write the instructions down before I had time to respond.

I had been pushed too far. I spoke before they had time to question me. "According to the Edgar Cayce readings," I said with authority, "the castor oil pack seems to have a more profound effect when used on consecutive days." My words were slow and deliberate. They looked at me with some degree of astonishment.

"And how do you know this?" one inquired.

"Because I have been studying the Cayce readings since I was twelve years old," I replied. "I think it's wonderful that you are teaching the Cayce therapies at this school," I went on. "If you're going to use them, I think it's a good idea that you be familiar enough to prescribe them correctly." My words were somewhat sarcastic, and I'm sure I wasn't acquiring any good karma at this moment. "Castor oil packs will definitely help this woman's immune system. They'll improve the quality of her dreams and help her see more clearly what the root of her difficulty is. But my personal experience with castor oil packs and the readings both suggest that consecutive nights are far more profoundly effective than alternating nights. If I am partly responsible for the outcome of this patient, I must insist that we use the consecutive nights on the castor oil packs. If the patient doesn't get results, but we're not using the treatments that I suggest, I do not want my grade to be based on the outcome of your chosen treatments." Again we were silent as we stared at each other in disbelief.

"All right," said the male professor, "we'll have it your way. But you need to get a better attitude."

"Yes," I thought to myself, "and so do you," but I didn't have the nerve to say that out loud.

That night I went home and had a serious conversation with myself about what it was that had happened in clinic that day. My attitude had gone from enthusiastic certainty about what my patient needed to a near all-out argument with two of my professors. It was not what I intended. I wanted to be a good student, I really did. Even when I thought I was doing an excellent job, I was harshly scolded. What was the problem? The answer was somewhat consoling, but not entirely.

I had chosen to go to naturopathic medical school because I could learn most of the conventional treatments, drugs, minor surgery that were necessary to practice medicine today. I could also learn the Edgar Cayce therapies: spinal manipulation, nutrition, herbs, mental hygiene, hydrotherapy, massage. I was learning the treatments recommended by Edgar Cayce. What I hadn't realized was that my naturopathic medical school, though they were teaching the therapies of Edgar Cayce, didn't really know who Edgar Cayce was. Branching out into the spiritual, the religious, and the metaphysical was a little beyond what they were prepared to accept. Furthermore, because naturopaths are not fully accepted "scientifically" in every state, the profession is entirely on its guard. It would be too risky to dabble in subjects that are as yet unproven. Someone could use that against us to show that we were "woo-woo" and not genuinely scientific. Although I was learning the therapies espoused in the Cayce readings, the school did not really know of Edgar Cayce and was not willing to make that spiritual/metaphysical/philosophical leap. I had to appreciate that. I would learn what I needed to learn to be a Cayce-inspired physician. The question was, would they conjure up the courage to acknowledge the higher truths about who we are as human beings? There was some sense of emptiness in my soul as I contemplated the question.

The people whom I had been surrounded with in medical school were no doubt spiritually inspired. In fact, our first course in philosophy talked about the "vital force," which can be equated to the "chi," "energy," "spirit"—whatever we call it from our own religious perspectives. I knew the teachers understood this. There was a lack of willingness to admit it more, to talk about it more, and that saddened me. If we acknowledge the Vital Source, the energy of God within us publicly, somehow the thought is that we're not scientific, we are "far out." And our profession at this point, in the minds of many, can't afford that sacrifice. Therefore, I had to "keep a lid" on that information. I would do my best, I determined, to talk about, to cultivate, and to acknowledge the spiritual aspect of our lives at every turn. On the other hand, I still wanted to graduate from medical school so that I could practice naturopathic medicine. I would do whatever I needed to do to accomplish those ends. I had come too far to give up my dream for someone else's lack of understanding.

I finished my third year of school, mostly with honors in academic subjects and a passing grade when it came to seeing patients. I believed it was my rebellion at the established norm that had handicapped my clinical grades. I determined that I would be the best I could be in my fourth year, that I would get honors when it came to patient care. The best of what my professors wanted me to be, I would be. I was newly dedicated to my cause.

Just before the end of my third year, I got a phone call from my parents. It was my mother who spoke first. "Dad's going in for more tests next month," she told me.

"For what?" I wanted to know, as terrible visions raced in my head.

"Well, he's just having some problems walking," my mother said. "Ever since we moved down here, the problems have been getting worse."

"Dad," I demanded, knowing he was on the other line, "what's going on here?"

"Oh, it's nothing, really," my dad answered in his characteristic way.

"Give me a break, Dad. This is me you're talking to. C'mon, I'm studying to be a doctor. Tell me what's wrong, maybe I'll know how to fix it." My tone was half-joking, but wholly serious.

"Well, I just hurt so bad in my lower legs," my dad told me, "and my back hurts, too. I can't really feel my lower legs, so it's hard to walk."

"How long has this been going on?" I questioned, now assuming my doctorly voice.

"It started soon after your Mom and I moved to Tucson," he told me.

I asked him a few more questions, the kind always asked when interviewing a patient. "Was there any injury that seemed to be the start of it? What was it associated with? What made it feel better? What made it feel worse? In what way did it limit you?" Etc., etc. I felt rather proud that I knew "the right questions" to ask. After our "telephone interview," I made my dad this offer: "Dad, I have an idea. Let me come and spend a month with you and Mom this summer. I think I know some things that may be helpful to your condition. If you get better, my fee will be next year's medical school tuition paid for—not a loan, no strings attached. If you don't get better, well, you're still out my board and room for a month. What do you say?" I knew they'd want me to come, if only for a visit.

"Oh, we could never ask you to do that," my mom piped in. "That would be too much to ask."

"You didn't ask," I reminded them. "I volunteered. Besides, what have the doctors offered you so far?"

"Well," my dad said slowly and hesitantly, "the doctor says I might need to have my vertebrae fused."

"Yes, and what will that do?" I queried.

"They're not sure," he said. "In fact, they still don't even know what's wrong with me. They said if I have the bones in my back fused, it might take away the pain. There's a fifty-fifty chance."

"Dad," I tried to reason with him, "does that sound like a very good set of odds to you?"

"No, actually I told them no, that I needed to talk to you first," my dad confessed. And didn't that make me feel good to know that Dad wanted to talk to me first! Finally, perhaps he was considering me to be a "real doctor."

"So what do you say, Dad? A month in Tucson. We do some treatments. If you get better, you pay for next year." I laid it on the line.

"Well," my dad responded, "your mom and I would sure like to have you visit."

"Dad," I said, "it would be far more than just a visit. I'm talking about things like a very precise daily diet, exercise program, massage . . . you'd have to agree to follow my therapies or I won't know if they work."

"Well, yeah, I couldn't really ask that of you, daughter," my dad replied.

"Dad, you didn't ask. I volunteered. I love you. I want you to be well. And I know that spinal fusion probably isn't going to help, particularly since no one even knows what's wrong with you yet. Just let me try the stuff I know. I'd be glad to see if it worked. Either way, it's going to cost you about the same, whether you need to have surgery or my treatment. And if it works, wouldn't you rather pay for another year of medical school," my question seemed so reasonable.

"Yes, I would," he admitted. And we made plans for me to visit.

What a great way to spend a month of summer, I thought to myself as I packed my suitcases! My parents had moved to Tucson, Arizona, less than one year earlier. I knew they had a swimming pool and a comfortable house. For me it would be both a vacation and a learning experience. I also was optimistic that my month of time would help my dad heal. And after that, it would pay for my next year's tuition! All in all, an offer too good to refuse.

It was good to see my parents. Their house was lovely. I'd have a good tan in a month's time and enjoy my visit with them. More important, I felt strongly that my father could be helped.

Dad was scheduled to have a CAT scan in two weeks. The orthopedic surgeon was still unclear as to the correct diagnosis, hence the need for the additional test. I had not completed my studies of neurology in school yet, but I read through the text with diligence before I examined my dad. By the time I was finished reading, my skill level had improved dramatically. The first day I was there, I performed a series of simple tests on my father, asking him to bend this way and that. To lift this and that in order for me to see what hurt. After about an hour of examination, I announced my diagnosis to him. "Dad, I told him, you have bone spurs on your lower lumbar spine. They're pushing on the nerves that supply your legs and that's why you have the numbness in the lower part of your feet and legs. Part of that change is due to your diet and exercise level and that we can work with pretty easily. In order to resolve the inflammation, we'll have to do some special exercises, some Epsom salt packs, and some castor oil packs. Now, what else is going on?" I asked him point blank, knowing he would probably not be able to answer.

"What do you mean?" he questioned me.

"Well, Dad," I explained, "by now I know that there's a mental or emotional contribution to your illness. We have to find that, too, or you won't get better from my best physical treatments. So what's going on?" I wanted to know.

"Nothing. I'm happy," my dad assured me. "I love your mother, we have a wonderful house . . . " he listed all the things that were right in his life.

"Let's look at it this way," I pressed on. "You started to feel the symptoms after you retired and moved to Tucson. Now what's been different?" Sometimes I find when I ask a question directly, it tends to jog the memory. My dad knew I wanted to help him and maybe that improved his ability to be honest and straightforward.

"Well, there is one thing that is different," he acknowledged, "but I don't think that's it."

"What's different, Dad?" I wanted to know. "What's different since the symptoms started, because that could be a key to the problem."

To my surprise he told me fluently and concisely: "When I was working, I was always so busy. People depended on me and I had lots of people whom I was responsible for helping. Since we've moved down here, there isn't that much to do. I clean the pool, keep the yard up, I'm going to redo the roof. But it's not really much activity in comparison. Maybe it's my level of physical activity that's been different," he suggested as a diagnosis.

"Yes, I'll bet that's part of it," I agreed with him, "but I think there's more. Dad, you and I both know that you have an incredible amount of talent. You've acquired skills that can only be gained through a lifetime of both experience and intelligence. Before you retired, you were using all of those resources to advantage. Now you've retired and what are you 'about'? Who gets the advantage of all this knowledge and experience?" I answered it for him, "Nobody. You've got all this wisdom and talent that's going to waste. It's stagnating, just like the discs in your lumbar vertebrae, Dad." Then I told him in all sincerity, "You still need to be working. Only now the difference is that your work is volunteer. You don't have to look over your shoulder to see how much money you're making from doing it. Now you get to give all this talent away for free, just for the joy of doing it. You will never be happy if you're not serving other people." In that moment of his diagnosis, he and I both knew what was true.

For one month my mom, dad, and I followed a fairly scheduled routine. Our diet was precise, both what I had learned in medical school and from the Cayce readings. In truth, the two were the same, though they may not have known that at school. Every morning before breakfast, we went for a walk to a local high school and then we ran up and down the bleachers. After getting home, we had a breakfast of specially made juices and some whole grain cereal. We lived, ate, and breathed good health and correction of the difficulty. Every afternoon I gave Dad a massage concentrating on the areas that were a problem. We did Epsom salt packs, and I prescribed special exercises for him. After two weeks, his symptoms were still present, and it was time to go for his CAT scan.

I accompanied him to the clinic where the scan was performed. I watched with the technician as the scan pictures came up on the monitor. After the test was over, my dad emerged from the room and the orthopedic surgeon appeared. "Mr. Wishmeyer," he announced, "we now have a more accurate diagnosis about the cause of your complaint. It seems that you have bone spurs on your lumbar vertebrae," he announced authoritatively. Without hesitation, my father said, "Oh, I knew that."

"How did you know?" the surgeon demanded. "We only just discovered that on the CAT scan," he reminded my father.

"Well," my dad told him, with a hint of pride in his voice, "this is my daughter. She's studying to be a naturopathic medical doctor. She came here two weeks ago, performed some tests on me, and then told me what you have just told me. I knew several weeks ago what my diagnosis was."

The surgeon looked at me quizzically and asked in a kindly tone, "What medical school are you going to?" The million-dollar question for all doctors.

I answered him straightforwardly, "The National College of Naturopathic Medicine."

"Where's that?" he asked in a tone that was quite changed.

"In Portland, Oregon," I responded and then added spontaneously, "it's the oldest college of naturopathic medicine in the country."

"And what's naturopathic medicine," his entire demeanor had changed, becoming somewhat sarcastic.

"It means that I study the same things that all doctors study in school," I told him. "And in addition, I'm a specialist in certain other therapies, including good nutrition, spinal manipulation, massage, hydrotherapy, homeopathy, herbal medicine, et al." We stared at each other in silence. I had come to recognize this silent stare since second grade.

"Well," he shook his head, "Mr. Wishmeyer, you have bone spurs on your lumbar spine. I recommend that you have surgery to remove the spurs and have your lumbar discs fused. I see no reason to wait on this surgery—the sooner, the better."

My dad asked in humble tones, "Now remind me what are the odds that this surgery will help my symptoms?"

"About fifty-fifty," the doctor said.

"And what does that mean, exactly?" Dad pressed.

"Well, it means that it may help your symptoms, or it may not," the surgeon responded.

"I see," said my dad. "Well, I think I'll just continue this treatment that my daughter has started, and I'll be in touch with you after she leaves."

We left together, and I could sense a new level of pride in my dad's voice and walk. Though he wasn't necessarily convinced about the kind of medicine I was studying, he had at least been encouraged by my accurate diagnosis. With odds of fifty-fifty, meaning it might help or it might not, he was willing to continue to give my treatment a try. At the very least, I could tell that he appreciated talking about retirement. Being retired with nothing to do didn't suit him. He knew it and I knew it. It was unlikely that his orthopedic surgeon would mention that subject to him, but we both knew it was important.

For another two weeks, we did our "homework." By the time I left Tucson, three important things had happened. One, Dad was no longer in pain and could walk and work in a normal way. Two, it had become apparent to him that retirement could not mean not doing much. If he were not actively helping people, he would not be satisfied. From now on for him, retirement would mean serving others. It was, I felt, a major turning point in his physical condition. And third, I had acquired something that every naturopathic student hopes for: the support and encouragement of one's parents. So often when we enter this profession, we are the "black sheep" of medicine. Because we're not licensed in every state, because we're not always covered by medical insurance, many times our parents and those near and dear to us accuse us of not being "real doctors." We know that we're as real as they come, but it's always encouraging to have our loved ones support our decision. With my dad newly recovered from an "incurable illness," I had their firm support in this chosen direction. It felt better to me than I can tell you. I was thrilled to have helped my dad. And now, my last year of medical school would not be a loan, but a gift.

Fourth year of medical school was the hardest and best year of school ever. I had vowed to myself that I would receive honors for my clinical studies—for seeing patients. While other students complained of not seeing enough patients, I was always booked. At night I would study patient cases and stories, thumbing through books and research articles to determine the cause of the difficulty and the best course of action. I threw myself into my work and my studies. As before, I did well in academic studies. I was crushed, however, when I received my first-term grade in fourth year clinic.

"P"—the sheet of paper read as it hung on the corkboard in the hall. "P" meant pass—O.K., satisfactory. I had passed my clinical studies, but not with honors. Why? I wondered. What could be wrong? I was one of the busiest students in the clinic. I recruited patients, and they came back to see me; my patient numbers were not a problem. Many of my patients recovered their health. Wasn't that a mark of a successful physician? Out of every student in my surgery class,

I performed more surgeries than anyone. My first surgery was on someone's face. I remembered that my hands trembled. But four months later when he showed me the scar, it was invisible. I had done another procedure on a patient that none of my professors in clinic had been willing to supervise. I had had to go outside the school to recruit a very old naturopath who was willing to oversee my performance of a delicate minor surgical procedure. In my heart I knew, in fact, that I deserved an "8" (honors grade). I had received only a pass. I was crestfallen.

To add further insult to injury, I received the actual numbers grade on our clinic evaluation sheet. Not only had I received a "pass" instead of an "honors," but I received a low pass grade. The numbers suggested that I passed only by the "skin of my teeth." I was upset, angry, furious, and confused. I made an appointment to see the dean of clinical education. Once in his office, my voice was pleading.

"Dr. Jones," I demanded of him, "look at this," as I pushed my grade record in front of him. "You've worked with me in clinic before. You know the quality of my work. I'm trying so hard to be an excellent student in clinic. This grade says that I have barely passed. What's wrong?" I pleaded. "What am I not learning or doing?" I pleaded again. "One of my teachers said I wasn't very good in physical diagnosis and, Dr. Jones, I know that's a lie. I've tutored classmates of mine who were failing clinical diagnosis class. I taught them how to do a complete physical exam, and they passed with honors; and now I, the one who tutored them, barely passes. I just don't understand. Can you tell me what this is about?" I was sincere, and I knew that Dr. Jones would level with me.

"Dana, it's what I call the 'red sports car phenomenon,' and I believe you're suffering from it."

I looked at him quizzically. I did not understand. He went on to explain. "What I see is that both you and Nigel (a medical doctor in my class obtaining his naturopathic degree) are suffering from it right now and I'm sorry for you both. Here's the fact. If an old brown station wagon and a bright shiny new red sports car are both exceeding the speed limit down the highway, who do you think will get the ticket?" His question was simple and direct.

"The red sports car, of course," I answered without hesitation.

"Yes, of course," he confirmed. "The policeman can only stop one car, and the one that's the flashiest and most obvious will be the one to get the ticket. You always stand out to your professors. If you disagree with them, you say so. You'll argue with them and stare them straight in the eyes. You're a red sports car. And so is your classmate Nigel. As a medical doctor with years of experience, he's quite good with diagnosis. He doesn't always understand naturopathic philosophy or treatment, but at diagnosis, he's quite good. He does the same thing you do—he'll argue, he'll object—he's a red sports car. I don't think the professors could fail you because all of us work with you and know the quality of your work. But they might if they feel irritated enough, make it very difficult for you to graduate. You're a red sports car, and you're going too fast for them. You're always the one who will get the ticket. If you want to make things easier for yourself, slow down. Talk more softly, lay lower, argue less. Even if you disagree with someone and you're sure you're right, be more humble. Can you do that?" he asked me.

"Dr. Jones," I told him without contemplation, "I can do whatever I need to do to graduate. I can lay flat on the ground with my face prone in the dust if I need to in order to become a doctor. I see this as a possible flaw in some of my professors, but it must also be a flaw in me. Cayce said to take each person at his or her level of consciousness. If one's level of consciousness says that I must be more humble, must not speak my truth, must give others only what they are expecting to hear and no more, I can do that.

You, as director of this clinic, must know that if I do that it is because I have chosen to in order that I might graduate successfully. It would be my preference to be able to debate and negotiate with all of my instructors. If I can't, I guess I can at least practice humility. Thanks for your help and your honesty."

I left his office with a feeling of greater understanding and some relief. My professors were teaching the therapies of Edgar Cayce and many of them didn't even know it. As a student, I could try and tell them, but I might be criticized for my efforts. What could I do? I revised my strategy. I would be a good student. Good, meaning I would do all of the things I was asked to do. And when I did more than they asked me to do, I would not make it apparent. I would learn my lessons, but I would not necessarily attempt to teach, at least not yet. I would practice humbleness and humility. After all, wasn't that the supreme lesson of Jesus the Christ? Perhaps I did need more of that, much more of that than I had. I decided I would still be an honors student, whatever it would take.

"Best do it now," I thought to myself as I scheduled difficult patients and procedures in my appointment book. "If I can't perform this procedure with a skilled physician looking over my shoulder, then I'm quite sure I'll never do it when I'm on my own," I told myself. Even as a fourth-year student, I had patients who would come to see me from other places, other states. I would take into account their life-threatening illness, their extreme condition that no one had been able to solve. I reveled in the fact that I had great minds to consider the case with me. My professors—some lovable, some not; but all very skilled—were available to help me study each case. True to my decision, I finished my fourth year with honors in clinical studies. Toward the end of my fourth year, I had one last requirement to fulfill. All fourth-year students were obligated to work with other holistic doctors or clinics as part of their experience. I had never forgotten the vow I made to my parents, even before I started high school. "Some day," I told them, "I will work at the A.R.E. Clinic." I didn't know much about the clinic, except that it had the same name as the organization devoted to studying the Cayce readings—the Association for Research and Enlightenment, A.R.E. I also knew from my reading that the doctors at this clinic practiced treatments suggested in the Cayce material.

I made a phone call and wrote letters to the clinic and was accepted for a preceptorship. A preceptorship is a short, intense time of learning spent with a doctor or clinic. During the end of my fourth year, I flew to Phoenix to work at the clinic. Drs. Bill and Gladys McGarey were practicing at the A.R.E. clinic at that time. I enjoyed my experience there and seemed to fit in with their patients like a hand in a glove. "Why haven't we heard of naturopathy before?" they questioned me. "You know more about holistic healing than any other type of doctor I've ever seen," Dr. Bill would say. After two weeks of working at the clinic, I returned home to Oregon.

"How did you like Phoenix?" friends asked me.

"Well," I told them, "the clinic was fine, but I hate Phoenix. It's like the suburb of Hades. I would never want to live there. The only green you see are the trees and grass at the golf courses—it's awful." I am, you see, very attracted to trees and greenery and wildlife.

Graduation was a special day. All of us receiving our diplomas, being "hooded" with the traditional green hood of the physician. My parents and my favorite aunt and uncle joined me for the event.

After graduation, I had two important tasks facing me. One, I needed to take the national board exams and pass them in order to be licensed to practice medicine. Two, I needed to make a decision about where to go, where to practice, what to do. The first I knew how to accomplish.

The second, I was without ideas.

One day I went for a walk. It was only several weeks after graduation and two months away from taking the national board exams. "Lord," I prayed, "I have no direction, no certainty about which way to go. I want to do what You want me to do, but I don't know what that is. You have never spoken to me by etching Your message on the side of a rock with a lightening bolt. I have not heard voices or seen auras or sights or mystical revelations like Cayce or others. I have only a subtle intuition to depend on, and I don't feel anything right now. I have never seen You," I pleaded. "Which way shall I go?"

Every day following my graduation I made a full-time job of studying for my board exams. Most of my classmates had taken their basic science exams between their second and third year of medical school. Basic exams include physiology, anatomy, biochemistry, cellular biology, histology. In all, a total of six exams in the basic sciences are taken between second and third year of medical school. Because that was the time of my illness, I elected to postpone the exams. Now I was faced with taking all of the basic science exams plus the clinical exams at one time. A total of twenty-three examinations in four-and-a-half days. I had two-and-a-half months to study. I made it my full-time job.

One morning, before my studies began, I got up and went for a walk. "Lord, I want to walk in Thy way," I prayed, "but I don't know what that way is. I can see many things in the world, but I've never seen You. How do I know what You want me to do? I've had signs, but never strong signs. How do I know which to walk or to go?" I pleaded to God to give me an answer. Because of my "religious upbringing" and because of the studies of many other religions that I had elected to undertake myself, I had the verses of many scriptures floating in my head. "In Him we live, and move, and have our being" (Acts 17:28) . . . I heard the words of St. Paul from the Bible. "That great being is all this universe" . . . I heard from the *Bhagavad Gita*. "From Him, the entire creation flows" . . . I recalled the words of the *Tao Te Ching*. "Everything that is, is comprised of atoms" . . . I heard Dr. Rose say methodically in chemistry class. "I and my Father are one," (John 10:30) Jesus said. And still I had no sense of direction, of continuity. I walked through a field and to a lonely country cemetery. At this time I lived out in the country, sixteen miles away from the medical school and the city . . . "out in the sticks," a lovely place. As I arrived at the high mountaintop, I prayed out loud the prayer I had offered before. "Lord," I said, "I want to walk in Your way, but I don't know what that way is. I have never seen You, I have never touched You. How can I know Your way when I've never experienced You? I can see other people, I can touch other people, but I have never seen or touched You."

Suddenly in the moment of my prayer, the sun broke from behind a distant mountain peak. The rays of light flowed through the atmosphere like honey-colored fingers. As they touched me, I somehow had a revelation. "In Him we live, and move, and have our being," I heard St. Paul again. "I and my Father are one," Jesus said. "All things are comprised of atoms," I heard Dr. Rose's voice and then I knew. "O Lord," I prayed with both joy and humility, "all my life I have said I have never seen You. Now I know. I have never seen anything *but* You my whole life." All of a sudden every religion that I had ever read about made sense. Jesus said, "I and my Father are one" and everything that is, is one with the Father—of course! Dr. Rose said, "Everything in material existence is made of the one same stuff"—of course. "Out of this being, the entire universe flows," says the *Gita*. Of course. Everything that is, is made of the "God stuff." Just like every bit of ocean is comprised of the characteristics of the whole. A drop of the ocean could say, "I am the ocean." It would not, of course, be the entire ocean, but

BELOW: Me at two hours old. My mother's bargain with God to spare my life was successful.

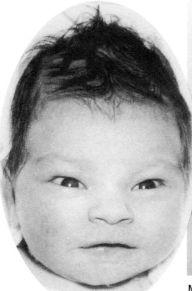

Me at three months, modeling for the "Wide Awake Answering Service."

RIGHT: Mom, Dad, and me—a happy family on Christmas morning.

BELOW: Grandpa and me, hard at work.

ABOVE: Grandma June in the '60s, and later (rt.) in the '70s, not long before she died. Like Cayce, Grandma had "the gift."

LEFT: Edgar Cayce, whose work is the basis of the Association for Research and Enlightenment, Inc.

BELOW LEFT: My mom and dad, newly wed, at home. Our house (behind them), built by my "new dad," would later burn to the ground.

The three of us again (my mom, dad, and me) when I was thirteen.

Lisa B. Before, during, and after she got on a "path to the top."

BELOW: Cody and a friend, back in the "old days" when he was blind.

BELOW: Now Cody writes his own letters to me. With this picture the note said, "Here's lookin' at ya', Doc!"

ABOVE: Me, teaching Max to dance "The Lord's Prayer."

LEFT: During talent night at the Ms. Senior Arizona Pageant, Max held the audience spellbound.

ABOVE: Max was genuinely surprised when she won the "Best Talent" award for her rendition of the dance.

LEFT: Me and Max backstage. I felt like a proud parent to have seen her go from a "crippled-up little old lady" to an award-winning dancer!

it would be a part of the ocean. In that moment I fell on my knees, laughing and crying. Laughing to have realized another truth and crying to have realized that this truth was always so present that I never saw it before. Everything that is, is God. Jesus did His best to tell us that. Edgar Cayce did his best to tell us that. The scripture of every major world religion tells us that. Our science tells us that. No matter what direction we approach, we find that. And yet, we hear it, we see it, we understand it not. And suddenly, I understood. My joy, my sorrow was profound. I fell on my knees laughing. "God, God," I prayed, "I said I have never seen You. Forgive me. I have never seen anything *but* You. Now everything that I learned makes sense. What would You have me do?" My prayer was sincere.

I heard a voice. It said, "You would *never* move to Phoenix?" I was silent, waiting for what would follow. "If you would never move to Phoenix, then I ask you, not even for Me?"

"Yes, Lord, for You," I said aloud. "For You I would go."

"Then go," the voice said. I walked home wondering how I would fulfill that instruction.

I was trained in most all of the Cayce therapies simply by virtue of my naturopathic background. They'd never had a naturopathic doctor at the clinic in Phoenix before. It seemed like a logical place to work, I told myself. If I'm supposed to go to Phoenix, that must be where I should go. I sat down to write a letter to the clinic administrator. What would I say? I wondered as I sat with pen in hand. "You yourselves acknowledge that a naturopathic doctor by virtue of training knows more about the Cayce therapies than any other kind of doctor?" Should I make a bold statement like that in the beginning of the letter? "And you've never had a doctor like this before at your clinic? When would you like me to start?" I pondered the content of my letter as I sat, pen poised over paper. Before I could begin writing, the telephone rang.

9

THE HEALING BEGINS

The voice on the other end of the phone was sweet, if surprising. "This is Cynthia," she said, "administrator of the A.R.E. Clinic. We don't know what you intend to do now that you're graduated, but I'd like to offer you a job. Would you be interested in working at the A.R.E. Clinic?"

My delight must have been evident to her from my voice. "Thank you for calling me now and not two hours from now," I remarked sincerely. "I was sitting down to write you a letter telling you that I thought you should hire me. Yes, I would be interested in a job. I've been thinking that I should come there."

I served at the A.R.E. Clinic for three years, both as a staff physician and as director of medical residencies. After three years of working at the Clinic, I transferred my energies to the Scottsdale Holistic Medical Group in Arizona, the office owned and operated by Gladys McGarey, one of the founders of the A.R.E. Clinic. I spent nearly a year as staff physician there, providing patient care and learning more about holistic medicine.

Most recently the "universal forces" have directed me in my ongoing private practice. The patients' stories and cases that follow in this book have come from my work as a medical student at the National College of Naturopathic Medicine, as director of medical residencies at the A.R.E. Clinic, as an associate at Scottsdale Holistic Medical Group, and from my private practice.

The importance of these patients is severalfold. Number one, these are real people—people whose stories have been seen, observed, and recorded. If they sound similar to your own case, so be it. Their stories are designed to encourage, to inspire, and to enlighten you. Two, these stories are not meant for medical diagnosis. No two beings are exactly alike; no two people require the same treatment. You should consult your own holistic practitioner for advice and recommendations regarding your care. The stories, however, are meant to remind you that cure is always possible. Further, if you see in these pages the face of your own divinity, then I am doubly grateful.

Be well, be happy, be healthy. Most of all, may you always "remember who you are."

Part

2

10

WHAT YE EAT
AND WHAt YE THINK

The young woman in the room was pretty, but quite frail looking. "Panic attacks" were listed as her chief complaint. The patient, Beth, was the mother of two small children. She was, by her own report, happily married for the last eight years. Her complaint was frequent and overwhelming attacks of anxiety, which she also described as "severe panic." She would feel these episodes first thing in the morning upon arising, with heart palpitations and jitteriness. The symptoms improved somewhat during the day, and she felt best when she was working. Driving on the highway in a car would cause such total panic that she had virtually ceased to drive. She also had difficulty sleeping at night, which had started when the panic attacks began.

Like many people who suffer from anxiety disorders, no external cause was obvious. There were no job stresses, relationship stresses, money difficulties, or other factors that explained her intense anxiety. Endogenous (meaning internally generated) attacks can be particularly frustrating to the person who experiences them. The symptoms can leave patients feeling extremely helpless and out of control because they are not even able to recognize the cause of their difficulty. Although anxiety attacks that seem connected to external events are also frustrating, they tend to be, as a rule, somewhat less frightening to the people who experience them. In Beth's circumstance, this was not the case.

Beth had been evaluated by multiple psychiatrists and other physicians. No physical cause or contribution to her difficulty had been found. Her psychiatric evaluation was also largely unremarkable except to note her symptom—the anxiety attacks. One of the things that she told me numerous times during our first visit was that she wondered if she were crazy. When I asked her why she thought this might be a possibility, she said it was because no cause for her symptoms had been found. "Maybe I'm just making these symptoms up," she told me forlornly, almost as a question.

"Well," I pointed out to her, "almost everyone who has a physical illness has a mental contribution to that illness. Whether the mental contribution came first or second is sometimes hard to know, but it is virtually always present. You may be generating or contributing to this difficulty with your thoughts, and it's very important that we explore that together. We must also continue to look for any as-yet-undiagnosed physical contributions to the illness. There are some things that can cause this type of symptom that have not yet been ruled out by the other physicians who have examined you. We'll look at the difficulty from all angles and see if we can find out why *you*, in particular, are having this problem. Your circumstance will be a little different than anybody else who's experienced this before. We can rely on other people's experience as a guideline, but each of us is unique. That can sometimes make diagnosis a little more challenging, but we won't let it dissuade us."

She gave a wry smile for the first time since the beginning of our visit. It was that tentative look of hope that people sometimes get after feeling hopeless for a long time.

Because she had been seen and evaluated by so many physicians, all of her laboratory tests were available and up to date. There was nothing of remarkability on any of her blood or lab studies. No chart notes reflected any difficulty or unusualness on the physical exam, but I always like to do some physical examination myself. I never know what another physician has been looking for. In addition to the conventional ways of examining a body, I also include some diagnostic signs from other healing symptoms, such as feeling pulses and looking at the tongue from a Chinese medicine perspective and examining the irises of the eyes for iridology signs. Because of this, I suggested that we have a brief physical examination at our next visit. In the meantime, I asked Beth to keep a diet and symptom diary for me. For five days, she was to write down everything she ate, including the times, and what was going on around her. I also asked her to record any symptom as it occurred, again noting the time and surroundings. In the interim between our next visit, I went through all of her previous records and studied her case.

There was one thing I saw that I could do to help Beth right away. Studying her symptoms, I realized that a particular homeopathic remedy emerged as being indicated. One of the nice things about homeopathy is that you do not have to have a diagnosis in order to make a prescription. In conventional medicine, because we are working on the physical level we must first try to identify the physical imbalance. When we are able to do so and wind up with a disease that has a name, then we know what medicine to give. For the many folks who have complaints but no clear diagnosis, a correct prescription becomes more challenging. In homeopathy, however, remedies are prescribed on the basis of symptoms alone. The name of a particular disease is unimportant in making a homeopathic recommendation. Except to call Beth's problem "anxiety attacks," there was no clear diagnosis available. Her symptoms suggested a particular homeopathic remedy, however, and I determined that I would start her on that at our next visit.

Also, in studying her records, it became apparent to me that low blood sugar had never been ruled out. Low blood sugar, also called "hypoglycemia," is sometimes underappreciated as a diagnosis. While some doctors recognize this as a bona fide difficulty, many others say that it is "not a real problem." The criteria used to diagnosis hypoglycemia exclude a lot of people who probably actually suffer from the disease. When the body's level of blood sugar drops low, the adrenal glands will release adrenalin in an attempt to compensate. Adrenalin, the "fight-or-flight hormone," causes an increase in heart rate and breathing. We're all familiar with the symptoms we get when we're frightened. That same set of symptoms occurs when the adrenal glands are stimulated from any cause. Therefore, a drop in blood sugar, which can cause a release of adrenalin, can mimic the "fight-or-flight" symptoms. An anxiety or panic attack is described by those who experience it as being the same as this "fight-or-flight" mechanism. The only difference, in Beth's case and in others, is that no cause can be explained. No matter how they become stimulated, the adrenal glands will cause this "fight-or-flight," anxiety-attack set of symptoms. Because low blood sugar can initiate the cycle and because it had not yet been ruled out in Beth's case, I wrote it on my list as something we would need to explore.

When I saw her the following week, she had her diet and symptom diaries confidently in hand. She had kept a very accurate track, just as I had asked her to do. A quick glance at her diet further convinced me of the importance of ruling out low blood sugar. Her breakfast was meager; her daily fare was filled with refined sugar, and she tended to eat very little dinner in the evening after having prepared it for her family. When I questioned her about this, she told me that she just wasn't hungry. Next I asked her about some of the things that made her afraid. "I don't mean necessarily when you have your panic attacks," I said, "just in general. What things really get you stirred up?" Some of the things that bothered her included a fear that she was going crazy. Every time she had a panic attack that she couldn't explain, her fear of going crazy increased. The other thing that made her fearful was the possibility of passing out while driving on the highway. She would get so nervous, she told me, that she was afraid she would lose consciousness while driving. "Has this ever happened to you before?" I questioned. "No," she said, "it hasn't." But she feared it nonetheless.

There was one other thing that tended to make her worry. She was afraid of what might happen to her children when they grew up. When I questioned her about this, she said that "with all the evil in the world, I'm afraid they might not turn out right."

"Are you having any trouble with them now?" I inquired.

"Oh, no," she said, "they're very good children and they're doing well in school. It's just that there's a lot of violence in the world and I'm always afraid of what will happen to them."

I reminded her that if she were doing the best that she knew as a parent and mother, attempting to give her children good values and a solid family background, the rest of what would happen to them was beyond her control. Hadn't she known families who were good and upstanding

that still had a child turn out bad? Yes, she said she had
known such families. And hadn't she seen families who were
troubled and difficult, but the children turned out fine? Yes,
she had seen that, too, she admitted. "Well," I summarized,
"you can only do the best you can do and beyond that, the
outcome may be in Higher Hands." I thought of Cayce's
words, "Why worry when you can pray." I asked her about
her faith, and she said she did have some remote spiritual
beliefs related to Catholicism. "I think perhaps it would help
you to continue doing the best you can do as a mother and
beyond that to put the outcome and the lives of your children in God's hands. That way, you won't be wasting any
valuable energy with worry and contributing to your own
physical difficulty. Besides, your worry does not improve the
circumstance. Worrying does not help the outcome. It's a
waste of energy. But your prayers are a *positive* use of that
same energy that will actually have an effect in helping protect your children." This made sense to her, and she agreed
to begin the practice of prayer in substitution for worry.

There is a way to test for low blood sugar. It requires feed-
ing a pure source of sugar to a patient and then taking blood
every hour for six hours to see what happens to the sugar
level. Unless I am uncertain about the diagnosis, I prefer
not to have to perform this test. First, if someone is indeed
hypoglycemic, the test can be very uncomfortable for that
person, as well as time consuming. Second, and most important, the test result may be within the normal range, but
the patient can still be having an abnormal response. In
other words, the test is not always diagnostic. This is because different individuals will experience symptoms at
different levels of blood sugar. One person's blood sugar
may be as low as fifty and he or she will feel fine, while someone else at a blood sugar level of fifty will be having all the
symptoms of hypoglycemia. Because Beth's diet was a
pretty Standard American Diet (S.A.D.) to begin with, she

would benefit, I knew, from some dietary changes. If the cause or contribution of her complaint was hypoglycemia, we would know it by a correction of the diet, thus avoiding the cumbersome and uncomfortable test.

I explained to Beth why we needed to change her diet in order to rule out dips in blood sugar. "How would blood sugar problems cause an anxiety attack?" she wanted to know.

"Good question," I asked, "and I think it will help you to know the answer." I explained the mechanism to her: that when blood sugar drops, the adrenal glands "kick in" in an attempt to compensate. The effect of adrenalin in the system is the fight-or-flight reaction which, as most of us know, is an anxiety response.

"And the reason my symptoms are worse in the morning?"

"Well, your diet diary shows that you don't eat much in the way of dinner," I pointed out. "Then, during the night, you go for a full eight or nine hours without any additional food. By the time you wake up in the morning, your blood sugar is probably at an all-time low. Again, in an attempt to give you enough blood sugar to get you out of bed, your body may be secreting adrenalin from the adrenal glands. A big blast of adrenalin will cause heart palpitations, sweating, and all of the symptoms that you've described to me. All of the more worrisome difficulties that could cause this syndrome have already been ruled out by various tests that have previously been performed. This one item has not been ruled out. If you're up for it, I suggest we make some significant dietary changes and see what effect that has on your symptoms."

Beth was agreeable to the dietary suggestions. Although she at first protested that some of them would be hard (almost everyone makes this protest at the beginning—we humans resist change), she agreed to give it her best effort.

Because she understood why and how her diet might be causing her symptoms, she was more highly motivated. Also, her symptoms had become severe enough as to interfere dramatically in her day-to-day living. Again, physical and emotional distress can also serve as a powerful motivator.

I recommended a diet that was more well-balanced, containing more protein, more fruits and vegetables, and whole grains in place of refined sugars. I also made a homeopathic prescription at the same time.

Finally, we talked about the contribution of thought to this difficulty. "It may be like a vicious cycle," I commented. "A fear thought can cause the release of adrenalin, which can lower blood sugar and cause more adrenalin, or a physical drop in blood sugar can cause the release of adrenalin which, once initiated, allows you to think your fear thoughts more easily. We don't know which comes first here: the chicken or the egg. We *do* know that your thought contribution of fear and worry will only aggravate your condition. When you get a panic attack, I want you first to have a little bit of diluted grape juice to improve your blood sugar. Secondly, I want you to sit down, take a few deep breaths, and mentally calm yourself. Remember, nobody can find any physical problem that is dangerous to you when you're having these attacks. So sit down and remind yourself that although you are uncomfortable, this situation is not thought to be life-threatening. Let's not add *more* fear on top of the *other* fear that you're already experiencing."

I taught her some relaxation techniques and suggested that she work with our resident psychologist to learn biofeedback and receive some counseling. Most of us, I believe, would benefit from knowing and practicing relaxation techniques.

When I saw her four weeks later, I thought that I had walked into the wrong treatment room. Her whole appearance and countenance were different. She sat up straight and confidently in the chair. The clothes she wore were brighter and bolder than I had ever seen. She'd put on some makeup and looked quite beautiful. She flashed a warm smile as I entered the room.

"Beth?" I said, somewhat amazed.

"Yes, hi, Dr. Myatt," she said. "I drove myself here today!"

"Well, tell me what's happened since I saw you last." I was eager to hear the story.

"Well, I'm feeling much better," she related. "I can drive the car on the freeway, and most of the time I feel just fine. Once in a while I get a little nervous, but I breathe deeply and remind myself that I'm going to be O.K. I also remind myself that the thing that I was afraid of before—passing out—has never happened and, therefore, probably never will. I also talk to myself and remind myself that I could pull over if things got really bad. Just knowing that, reminding myself of that, seems to calm me down.

"I've been following the diet that you recommended. It was a little difficult at first, but when I realize how much better I feel, it's getting easier and easier. One of my boys seems to have a problem with hyperactivity in school. I cook for the family the same way I'm cooking for myself, and his hyperactivity is much decreased, his teacher tells me. I think maybe he was having some kind of blood sugar difficulty as well. Do you think that's possible?"

"Oh, yes. Not only possible, but quite probable. Blood sugar difficulties are very often a big part of hyperactivity, also called Attention Deficit Disorder (ADD) in children. It might simply be that your previous diet was just not conducive to everyone's good health. Tell me what else has been going on for you."

"I don't have those palpitations in the morning. Oh, sometimes I feel a little fluttery. But if I get up, have my breakfast, and practice some deep breathing, I really feel good. Sometimes I take that homeopathic remedy you gave me right at the time I'm having symptoms, and that seems to help quite a bit. I'm sleeping much better at night. In fact, next time I see my psychiatrist, I'm going to ask him if he can take me off my other medication. I have a feeling that I may not need it any more."

"I think that's a very reasonable idea," I offered. "If the original difficulty has been corrected, you may not need those symptomatic treatments. Be sure you check with him as to how to wean off the medications, however. Don't just stop 'cold turkey.' Some medicines can be discontinued suddenly, others must be decreased slowly. The medicines you're on will best be decreased slowly, over time. Since your psychiatrist prescribed the medications, let's leave it to him to tell you how to do that. What about the worry you were experiencing relative to your children? Has that changed?"

"Oh, yes," she said, "I meant to tell you. I've started going to church more now. I'd gotten away from it for a long time. I thought about what you said that worrying doesn't help, but that praying might. So I decided that instead of worrying, I would save that energy and go to church and talk to God about the boys. You know, it really works. I feel much better about them now. I know I can only do the best I know how to do. I can try to shelter and shield them from some of the scary things that go on in the world, but I can't change the bigger picture, except maybe by my prayers. Anyway, since I've been praying for them, I find I really don't worry about them. I'm confident that they're going to grow up happy, healthy, and strong. I put their lives in God's hands and have gotten back closer to my religious practices. That feels really good to me. Even my husband is coming to church with me now and our relationship seems better, though it was always O.K."

It took a few additional months of "fine tuning" her treatment regimen to get Beth back to a normal state. Occasionally, she had some difficulty with sleep, but a nighttime castor oil pack seemed to help greatly with this. She can drive her car, go places, and do things like she could before. Her energy has also improved dramatically. Again—probably as a result of improving her blood sugar levels and her diet. Last, but not least, her thoughts about life have improved greatly. When a thought creeps up that is of a fearful nature, she has learned how to nip it in the bud by positive self-talk and prayer. In the old days, she would allow that fear to grow and magnify until it overwhelmed her. By learning a few new mental techniques, she has made a big difference in her own life.

Cayce said that what we eat and what we think, together results in what we are physically. In Beth's case, this certainly proved to be true.

11

Too Young to Be Old

"**A** feeling of desperation that borders on panic" is how Maxine described her mental state at our first visit. "The problem is *not* in my head," she explained, "but entirely in my body." At seventy-one years old, this spritely artist had become so crippled due to some "mysterious illness" that she was no longer able to paint and sculpt. Pain racked every part of her body, the joints and muscles of her legs and arms. The most severe pain was in her right shoulder. Being a right-handed artist, she was forced to stop the very art that she so loved. In addition to the musculoskeletal aches and pains, she had a disturbance in her intestines that left her with chronic, explosive diarrhea and gas and bloating. She could scarcely leave home for fear that she would require restroom facilities at any moment. There was little left for her to do. Travel was impossible due to pain and her digestive problem. Staying home and practicing her art was impossible due to shoulder immobility.

"Max," as she preferred to be called, had seen numerous physicians, including several orthopedic surgeons. She had received extensive blood work, physical examinations, and CAT scans. Except for a slight calcium deposit in her right shoulder, nothing was found. Her last physician finally suggested that she take Valium®, a mood-altering drug that helps relieve anxiety. Essentially, she was told that the pain was imaginary. Contrary to that diagnosis, one doctor reminded her that, at her age, pain was to be expected.

But this is *not* what Max expected. Her attitude had always been youthful and optimistic. She had not planned to grow old this early, she told me. Finding little else to live for, she had decided to sell her house and take one final trip around the world before doing she-knew-not-what. The problem was that even such a trip seemed impossible. Her daughter, having heard about the work of Edgar Cayce, recommended that she go see a Cayce-inspired physician. Thanks to that recommendation, Max was in my office, seeming already relieved somehow just to know that someone would listen.

It is well known among naturally inspired physicians and anyone who has studied the Cayce readings that body aches and pains, what we generally term arthritis or rheumatism, are most often due to an acid/alkaline imbalance in the bloodstream. This is largely the result of a faulty diet and lack of sufficient activity. In examining Max's diet history, I found that her diet was extremely acidic, which, according to Cayce, is the opposite of what will make for good health. Because of her sensitive stomach and the gas, bloating, and diarrhea which followed the ingestion of many foods, she had severely restricted her diet—limiting it to starches and proteins—all acid forming. What she needed to be eating was more fruits and vegetables, but these foods seemed to irritate her gastrointestinal condition. She was stuck in what appeared to be a bit of a "catch-22."

Further questioning suggested that she had an overgrowth of yeast in her intestinal track. Some minimal laboratory testing confirmed this suspicion. It is interesting to note here that Edgar Cayce did not mention a frequent, modern-day difficulty called candidiasis. Candidiasis is an overgrowth of yeast that begins most usually in the intestinal track and causes problems everywhere in the body. In Edgar Cayce's day, however, the use of antibiotics and super-antibiotics was not nearly so widespread. Antibiotics, although at times lifesaving, can cause certain problems. In addition to the "bad" bacteria that they kill, they also damage the "good" bacteria in the intestines. Colonies of yeast, which also live in the intestines, can then grow rampant. I believe that this difficulty is actually much more prevalent now than it was in Cayce's time. There has been a great increase in the use of these antibiotics, increased levels of stress, and increased processing and consuming of unnatural foods—all of which can harm the normal G.I. bacteria. One of the main ways to treat this overgrowth of yeast is to modify the diet and give a product which is derived from the castor oil bean. I often use plain castor oil instead and get very good results. Although this difficulty was not more extensively described by Cayce, there appears to have been good reason for that. The treatment for it, I'm sure, would have delighted Cayce: several drops of castor oil by mouth, two to three times per day.

One of our first steps was to put Max on an anticandida diet. This excluded refined sugars, carbohydrates, and foods containing mold. Once we made this shift and began other treatments for the candida, her gastrointestinal condition

improved and she was able to eat more fruits and vegetables. The eight or more aspirin per day that she had been
taking to help control pain became a thing of the past.

One day, after Max was off all medication for her pain
and was doing much better, she appeared in the office for
an emergency visit. Suddenly, everything in her body had
"flared up." She ached all over, she could scarcely stand the
pain. "And what was suddenly different?" I asked. "Did you
change your diet? Did you go somewhere new? What's different?"

"Nothing's different," she assured me. "I've been on the
diet, I've been taking the castor oil and using the castor oil
packs. Nothing is different. I'm in so much pain today, I had
to have my grandson, Philip, bring me to the office."

"Your grandson?" I asked. "Does he live in town? I've
never heard you talk about him."

"No," she said, "he and Sally, my daughter, live out of state
but they are here visiting."

"And when did they get here?" I asked.

"Last night." The words were out of her mouth before the
realization struck. She looked at me with a wide-eyed curiosity and then shook her head no. "It has nothing to do with
that," she replied. "I love them; we have a good relationship."

"Interesting you should say that," I noted, "considering
that I hadn't asked you about your relationship. I want you
to continue doing everything that you are currently doing."
I gave her a homeopathic remedy, which Cayce said is better than pharmaceutical medicine, and asked her to think
about how her relationship with her daughter and grandson could somehow be related to the difficulty.

Cayce said, "Mind is the builder." I know that. If her mind
were disturbed by thoughts of or relationship experiences
with her children, that could be causing a problem. Although she didn't want to hear it, she went home with her
remedy and something to think about.

She called me the next day. She felt entirely well, no aches or pains. She had done her castor oil pack, stayed with her diet, taken the homeopathic remedy, and given the situation some serious thought. Yes, there was something in her relationship with her children. "Could it be contributing?" she wanted to know. It seems that her grown children were taking advantage of her, dropping in at any hour of the night or day without so much as a phone call, expecting that they would always be welcome, which they were, but showing little or no respect for her life. On their recent visit, the same thing had happened again. She found it very irritating. What she hadn't realized, but I was quick to point out, is that she found it irritating on more than just the mental level. Her irritation at this circumstance was reflected throughout her entire being. It was time to have a heart-to-heart talk with her children, explain to them how she felt, explain to them that she loved them, but would no longer tolerate their disrespectfulness.

Though all of this made some sense to Max, she still had difficulties with the idea. "After all, wasn't it the responsibility of a good mother to always love and welcome her children into her home?" she asked me.

"Oh, yes, to love them and to welcome them is a very nurturing thing to do. It is *not* unloving, however, to insist that they behave in mature and respectful ways." With a daughter that was close to fifty and a grandson in his mid-twenties, I suggested that she might be doing them a disservice to allow them to treat her with so little respect. "If you love them, you will help them see what they are doing," I assured her. "It is not unloving to give strong counsel to your children. That's called 'tough love.' The Bible says that even God chastises those whom He loves. You need to stand up for *yourself* as a child of God and help correct the thoughts of your children. Your physical difficulty, which in the past made you so sore that you couldn't stand, is a symbol for the problem. You just 'can't stand' this behavior any longer. Until you speak up for yourself, until you tell your children what is acceptable behavior toward you and what is not, you will continue to have relapses of aches and pains. Do with this information what you will, but I think it is the final ingredient that we need to get you better."

Max thought about our discussion and decided to act on it. She clarified her boundaries with her children and let them know that she was not available at all hours of the day and night for them to drop in with no phone calls and no minimal amount of respect that they would give anyone else. She said that she felt much better when she had done that. Miraculously, the last of her aches and pains subsided and she has had no acute flare-ups since that time.

There is only the faintest occasional trace of a discomfort in her shoulder—not nearly enough to keep her away from her art. She's back into painting, displaying her works in local galleries and shops. Her gastrointestinal distress bothers her only if she becomes entirely inattentive to diet, which she no longer does because she doesn't like the consequences.

She was surprised when I called her and told her that I'd seen a notice in the newspaper—a call for contestants in a senior beauty and talent pageant. I suggested that she enter.

"But I don't have a talent that presents well on stage," she argued. "It would be difficult to show my paintings, so what could I do?"

"I'll teach you a dance," I told her, "an interpretative dance to the Lord's Prayer."

The first time she saw the dance, she gracefully declined my offer. "Far too physical. I can't move like that," she protested.

But I protested further, "Yes, you *can* learn the dance. You *need* to learn the dance because it will help restore your physical strength. There is no reason why you are not able to do these movements." She reluctantly agreed, and over the course of an eight-week period she became masterful at a highly physical interpretation of the Lord's Prayer set to music.

Her performance in the pageant made me feel like a proud parent. During the "philosophy of life" section of the pageant, she described how taking each day as it comes while always looking to the Higher Power for guidance was her rule of thumb. She moved with the grace and elegance of a much younger woman. As the final announcement was made, she was in the top ten of the most talented, intelligent, successful, spiritually minded women in the state. And although she did not take a final trophy for beauty (though she is a beauty), her rendition of the Lord's Prayer won the "Best of Talent" award in the state finals!

With an enthusiastic hug backstage, she told me, "I knew I was too young to feel that old! Thank you for helping me find myself again. Thank you for helping me feel better again. Thank you for helping me reclaim my soul."

Follow-up:

Maxine has gone on to accomplish many noteworthy goals. First, she completed another oil painting titled "The Rose" and had a major art showing in Scottsdale, Arizona. Secondly, she and I now perform and teach "The Lord's Prayer" to groups around the country. We also work together to facilitate experiential programs in art, music, and dance.

Most important, she counsels folks on the value of "embracing life"—on doing whatever we can do regardless of age, handicap, or circumstance. Her life is a living testimony to the strength of the human body/mind. She is also a living example of what can be accomplished—*no matter what our age.* Cayce said, "Let age only ripen thee." Maxine can now show people just what that means.

12

HE ONCE
WAS BLIND BUT NOW . . .

The young man in the treatment room seemed a bit peculiar to me as I opened the door and stood looking. He was dressed in western-style clothing with a big, black Stetson hat and black sunglasses. On his belt loop was a beeper. As I opened the door, he seemed to look at me with his ears instead of his eyes. In fact, he didn't turn around at all as I entered, but cocked his head to the side, listening.

"Hello, I'm Dr. Myatt," I introduced myself with an outstretched hand.

"And you are?" I paused, waiting for him to fill in the blank.

"Cody," he answered with a bit of a drawl. "How ya doin',

doc?" He still did not turn his head in my direction. "I can tell where you are," he said, "but I'm blind, you see. Excuse me for not taking off my sunglasses. They do a good job of hiding my eyes."

"Let me show you where the chair is, Cody," I offered as I helped him find his seat. "Tell me your story." I settled into my own chair expecting this to be one of the more unusual cases. I was not disappointed.

Cody was young, only thirty-eight. He had been an insulin-dependent diabetic since age five. It was the diabetes followed by some unsuccessful laser surgery that had culminated in his near-total blindness. "Blind in one eye and can barely see light and dark in the other," he told me. "The opthalmologists have told me I will never see again. I think maybe they're wrong. I heard that you do acupuncture. I thought maybe with some treatment, we could bring back my eyesight."

"Well, anything's possible," I said. "Tell me more about yourself and your condition. That will help me know what things may be helpful to you in restoring your eyesight."

Though most physicians would call me foolish for encouraging a man in such a condition, I felt quite serious in my attempt to help him. Because I have seen miracles—people recovered when they were not expected to—I am willing to believe that other miracles are always possible. If a patient tells me that he or she is expecting a miracle, I am willing to participate. Foolhardy as it might have seemed to some, I pressed on with my questions.

"The diabetes has never been well controlled," he told me. "In fact, my kidneys have failed completely. I get regular dialysis." He held out his arm showing me the special catheter that had been implanted for that purpose. "Even the dialysis doesn't seem to be working well now," he explained. "I'm in line for a kidney transplant. The doctors think that because I'm young, I may be a good candidate. If

I had a new kidney, I wouldn't need dialysis any more. I'm really hoping they will find one for me."

"And the beeper?" I asked, pointing with a gesture, forgetting momentarily that Cody was blind.

"That's so the hospital can beep me if a kidney suddenly becomes available. It's on day and night. My wife also 'mans' the telephone," he said with a grin.

"Oh, tell me more about your family," I pressed on.

"I have a wife and three beautiful daughters," he said triumphantly. "I have a picture." Pulling out his wallet he offered a picture of three beautiful little girls.

"They're delightful," I said. "I hope I get to meet them."

"Oh, you will," he said. "I'll bring them with me one day. Are they beautiful? I know they are. I've never seen them though. I lost my eyesight just two months before the first one was born. I know they're beauties," he said lowering his head. I thought for just an instant that he might cry.

"Tell me again about your current blood sugar levels," I wanted to know. "What are the numbers like? Numbers are often important indicators to us 'doctor types.' "

"Well, my first morning sugar's around 300. I'll bring you all my recent lab reports. I get my blood work done every week for monitoring."

"It would also be helpful to me if you would keep a diet diary," I added. "If your blood sugars are still high, in spite of insulin, we may need to adjust your medications and dietary intake. Are you on anything special right now?"

"No," he said. "My doctor sent me to a nutritionist and she gave me sort of a general diet which I try to follow. I think I eat pretty well, but no one has really told me how I should eat to keep my sugar levels lower. Actually, I thought my blood sugar was pretty good."

"Well," I said, "your blood sugar is pretty high. Of course, it could be quite a bit higher. But if we're seeking improvement in your eyesight, I think we'll want consistently lower numbers. Send me a recent lab report and a diet diary and we'll see where we might be able to make some tune-ups or improvements in your routine. And now I'd like to examine you to get a sense of where we are at the beginning of this journey. Acupuncture might help and there may be other things that will also be important. Are you willing to work with other treatments in addition to the acupuncture?" I wanted to know up front what his level of motivation was.

"Yes, doc," he said again in that low drawl. "Whatever you say, I'll do. You're the first doctor who's been willing to talk to me about getting my eyesight back. All the others say I'm crazy—that it's hopeless. I'll listen to whatever you advise."

His physical examination was as remarkable as his story. Although he had lost nearly all the use of his kidneys, his muscles were still strong and firm. I remarked about his muscle tone, pointing out to him that physically he was quite solid. "I'm a martial artist," he told me. "A black belt in karate. I still work out a lot and I lift weights."

"Well, it's paid off and I hope you'll keep doing it," I responded. The pulses in his wrists and ankles were bounding. His blood pressure was quite high, an expected complication of advanced diabetes. The shunt in his arm looked like a super-huge vein. When I questioned him about it, he confirmed that it was somewhat uncomfortable.

His ankles and face were swollen with fluid. When I pressed my thumb against his shin, it made a deep indentation that took a long time to resolve. I suspected that his face would not be nearly so moonlike if he were in a more normal state.

And then there were his eyes. The left eye showed no response to light, and the interior part of the eye was entirely blocked by something. It looked as if a screen had been pulled down, surely and absolutely, just behind the pupil. The right eye, which Cody had told me still perceived some light, looked very similar to the left. I could not even begin to see the vessels in the back of the eyeball with my opthalmascope because the entire eyeball was filled with some substance. Again, it looked as if a screen had been pulled down right behind the pupil. When I told Cody what I saw, he mentioned that he had a large blood clot inside his eye. I questioned him about the possibility of surgical removal of the clot, and he told me that every eye specialist had told him that this would be impossible. When I shone the light directly into his eye, the pupil gave no response. "I thought you could see some bit of light and dark in this eye?" I questioned him.

"I can," he assured me.

"All right, I'm going to do a little test with you to get a sense of how much perception you have in this eye. When I'm shining the light directly in your eye, you tell me. When I take the light away, tell me that," I instructed him. Cody was unable to distinguish the difference between having a light shine in his eye and not. I pointed this out to him. "I thought you had light and dark perception?" I said. "But you can't distinguish the difference when I shine a flashlight in your eye and move it away."

"Well," he confessed hesitantly, "I think I have some light and dark perception, but it's really not very much."

"No, not very much at all," I reaffirmed for him.

"Cody, essentially what you are asking for is a miracle. I think, given the current state of your eyes, it would be a miracle for you to see again. Call me a cockeyed optimist, but I believe in miracles. I'm also willing to believe that sometimes we receive miracles when we're working very hard to invite them. In other words, help may certainly be possible for you and it will take something beyond what we know in conventional science to achieve it. I'm not willing to give away the resources on the physical level and only expect divine intervention. Have you ever heard the story about the born-again Christian and the flood?"

"No, I haven't," he grinned. "But I expect I'm going to."

"Yes, you are," I assured him, "but first, I suppose we should have an understanding. I'm willing to work with you in a situation that most people would consider hopeless. You will be expected to do your part in this, which will be most of the work. I will also expect you to listen to my jokes. Laughing at them is optional, but highly recommended." His grin was bigger this time and seemed to stretch all the way across his face.

"O.K., doc, I can handle it."

"Good, so here's the scene," I began. "There was a man newly born into his spiritual understanding. He hadn't had long to learn or study his new-found faith, but he was a believer. One day it started to rain. It continued to rain until the river rose and the town flooded. When the water was as high as his front door, a boat of Red Cross workers came by. 'Jump on in,' they said, 'we're evacuating; we'll take you to safety.' 'No, thanks,' he waved them on, 'I'm waiting for the Lord to save me.' 'Really,' they said, ' you should come with us. We're going to higher ground where you'll be safe.' 'No,' he refused again, 'I'll be fine.' The rain waters continued to fall. The first floor of his house was flooded. He was on the second floor of his house, peering out a window, when a second boat came by. 'Ho, friend,' a voice called from the boat. 'We're coming to get you. We'll take you to higher ground and you'll be safe.' 'No,' hollered the man from his second-story window. 'I'm waiting for the Lord to save me. I'll be fine.' 'You really must come with us,' the voice from the boat shouted again. 'It's expected to continue raining. The flood waters will only rise higher.' 'I'm fine,' said the man. 'My faith in God is strong and solid. I'm depending only on the Lord to save me.' The rain waters continued. Finally, the man was forced to stand on the roof of his home. Perched on the highest pinnacle of his house he saw a helicopter overhead. The helicopter flew low and dropped a rope out the door. 'Grab on, friend,' the voice shouted, 'and we will take you to safety.' 'No,' hollered the man, 'I'll be fine. I'm waiting on the Lord.' 'C'mon, buddy, grab the rope. The rain waters are expected to continue.' 'No,' the man shouted back, 'my faith is in God. I'm waiting for the Lord to save me and I know He will.' Reluctantly, the helicopter left. The rain waters continued and very soon the man was drowned. He found himself in a place of white light and great beauty. It was heaven and there incarnate he saw the Lord Himself. 'Lord, what am I doing here?' the man inquired. 'You died,' said the Lord, 'and now you're here.' 'But, Lord, I was waiting for You to save me from the flood waters. Why did I die? Why didn't You save me, Lord?' The Lord looked at him quizzically. 'Dear friend,' He said, 'I tried repeatedly to save you. I sent you two boats and a helicopter. What were you expecting?' "

"And the moral of that story," Cody said and paused, waiting for me to complete the sentence.

"Is," I chimed in, "that I would like you to be evaluated by an opthalmologist now at the beginning of treatment so that I can get an opinion of your current status. Let's know what all of our options are from any direction. I really don't care if it's acupuncture, surgery, diet, or a bolt of lightning that helps your eyes, you just want to be able to see again, right?"

"Right," he nodded and extended his hand in a gesture of handshake.

"Fine." I took it and shook it with both my hands. "I want to refer you to an opthalmologist for an evaluation. She's one of the very best in town. Let's see if any advances have been made in modern medicine that might have changed your possibility for some sort of surgery. That will also give us a baseline idea of what we're working with. Also, please keep that diet diary and get me the lab reports. I'm not going to needle you today—ha, at least not with acupuncture needles—until I have all of the data collected. Again, we've got a big task ahead of us, but I'm willing to believe in the possibilities if you are."

"That's all I'm asking for, doc," Cody reassured me. "Somebody to help me believe. I just want to see again."

A few days later I received the opthalmologist's report. In her opinion, there was nothing that could be done for Cody's eyesight. She acknowledged, however, that perhaps another specialist, a retinologist, might have some additional insight. She recommended that Cody consult another eye doctor. When I talked to Cody, he was reluctant. "Cody," I reminded him gently, but firmly, "we have to explore every possibility. Let's not miss the boat or the helicopter, because we're expecting something else. We need to know what could be done surgically and conventionally. Dr. Kay believes that this retinologist will know if there are any new treatments available that could help you. I recommend that you go."

"O.K., doc, I'm convinced," Cody said. "I just kind of hate to go because I know what they're going to say. It's the same thing they've always said. I'll go again if you think it's necessary."

The retinologist's report was the same. Cody's worst fears were acknowledged. "There is nothing that can be done for this man," the report stated. "A blood clot of the vitreous is so extensive that surgery would not be recommended. Also, the integrity of the optic nerve is in question. Even if the clot could be removed, there is a high probability that the optic nerve is dead. I do not recommend any treatment at this time except, perhaps, to refer the patient to the appropriate agencies for the handicapped to teach him to accept and deal with his disability."

I took a long deep breath and sighed. Somehow this report did not surprise nor disappoint me. At least I knew what Cody and I would be up against.

The following week our treatments began. First, I would assess Cody's pulses and tongue and then insert acupuncture needles at the indicated points. I also recommended to Cody that there was more that I thought was necessary in addition to the acupuncture. There were parts of his spine that were not moving well. These were the very areas where nerves would exit and supply the pancreas. I recommended a series of spinal manipulations, and our office visits would include both manipulative therapy and acupuncture. Edgar Cayce had mentioned in the readings which levels of the spine would need to be attended to. Interestingly, Cody's areas of difficulty were in the exact locations that Cayce had suggested.

We evaluated Cody's diet. He had not received sufficient counseling to understand the importance of careful dietary monitoring. With some guidance and training, we were able to achieve better blood sugar controls. By regulating his diet in conjunction with his insulin, his blood sugar levels dropped closer toward a normal range.

After working for several months on a regular and faithful basis, Cody failed to appear in the office one day. When I asked the office nurse if she knew why he wasn't there, she told me that he had been admitted to the hospital. A kidney had been found and he was going for his long-awaited kidney transplant. When I called the hospital, I found that the operation had been considered successful. Cody was still very groggy from the anesthesia and could not speak to me.

I didn't see him for several weeks. He was still in the hospital recovering from the arduous surgery of transplant. One day I got a call from his wife whom I had never met. Cody's body was rejecting the transplant and he had been put on the critical list. A heavy regimen of drugs had been prescribed to try to prevent the rejection of the new kidney. Cody's life hung in the balance along with the new kidney he had received. I would pray for him, I assured her, and I asked about whether or not she could "slip" him a homeopathic remedy. Homeopathy, you see, is not well known or accepted by conventional medicine. If we had asked permission to administer this remedy in the hospital, we almost surely would have been told no. Because the remedy was entirely nontoxic and would cause Cody no harm—only help—I recommended it to Cody's wife. Yes, she would be glad to try something—anything—and she would come by to pick up the medication from me.

The next several months were tenuous indeed. Cody was in and out of the hospital—more in than out. His body did not seem to be accepting the new kidney. He was having severe side effects from the immune-suppressing drugs being administered. The drugs, however, were necessary to allow his body to keep the new kidney. Finally, with very high doses of steroids, the graft rejection ceased. Cody was released from the hospital, and I saw him again in my office. His face was as round as a full moon. He was quite swollen with water, making him appear as if his skin would burst open from the pressure. Strong diuretics, prescribed by another of his physicians, were given to help counter the water retention, and this had changed the balance of minerals in the bloodstream. I was glad that Cody had a new kidney. For now, he was off dialysis. The side effects, however, were nearly as devastating as before the transplant. If we had made any headway before the surgery, we had a long distance to recover.

Just when it seemed that the situation was blackest, it got even blacker. Cody's wife left him and took the three children. She told him that the children deserved to have a father that wasn't sick all the time. Any good that might have come from the transplant seemed lost in light of this situation. Cody was absolutely devastated. Though he didn't talk of suicide, his moods became so bleak that I was concerned for his welfare. "Cody," I counseled him gently, "no one would deny that this is a terrible situation. I know your heart is broken to lose your family in this way. The kidney transplant was successful, and your body is starting to adjust to its new organ. Your life, or at least a part of it, has been saved in materiality. My heart breaks along with yours for the loss of your family, but your life must go on. You must find something interesting and joyful to do. We have to begin to climb out of this black hole and press on with life. Otherwise, what does it matter that your life was saved? If your life is not about something important, it doesn't matter. I want you to think about teaching again—teaching the martial arts to handicapped or disadvantaged children. You need to get your mind off of your own miseries. Help heal someone else's broken heart, so that you can heal your own."

There was no denying that Cody's situation was a sad one. After being given a new lease on life, he had lost his entire family. I knew and I tried to help him know that life does and must go on. Cody could not hear it or see it at that time and fell into a deeper pit of depression. He started to wallow in self-pity, to feel sorrier for himself than I had ever seen him. At this point, Cody and I had been working together for almost a year. Throughout his depression and recovery, we continued to do spinal manipulation, acupuncture, homeopathy, diet regulation, herbs, and our heart-to-heart talks.

Cody was in my office one day waiting for his appointment. After more than a year of treatment, I wasn't sure if I was helping him. At this point in his life, however, I knew that his office visits were important. To have someone to talk to, to help keep him grounded, to be a friend, was important. I had tried referring him to a counselor but he had never found anyone he felt comfortable with. In a sense, I was both his physician and his counselor, a role which I was comfortable with since it is really a part of being in family practice.

On this particular day, I saw a new patient right before Cody—a young woman of thirty-two who was paralyzed and in a wheelchair. An automobile accident years earlier had left her paralyzed from the neck down. Probably due to the paralysis, she was having recurrent urinary tract infections. She was in to see me to find out what could be done to help prevent these infections. The only treatment available from her allopathic physician was antibiotics. But each time she used the antibiotics, she would develop a secondary yeast infection. She wanted to know what her options were, hence her appointment with me. Throughout our discussions, I never heard her complain about her circumstance. A drunk driver had struck her car head on when she was in her late twenties, leaving her totally paralyzed. The only thing she had to hang onto was her mind. Her fiancé had been in the car with her and was killed instantly. I gave her my advice for preventing the infections that were bothering her, confident that they would help. Then I went to the next room and saw Cody.

Cody no longer needed dialysis as his new kidney was working sufficiently. Although he was having some side effects from the immune-suppressing drugs, he was physically doing much better. On the emotional level, however, he was still in a pit. I asked him if he had started looking into teaching opportunities, helping other people. No, he wasn't doing anything, he told me. Just sitting at home and thinking. "Sitting at home and thinking about your own troubles doesn't get the job done, Cody," I said with just a hint of sternness. "The only way for you to feel better about your sorry situation is to help someone else in a sorry situation. You just can't sit at home and wallow in your self-pity. Your family is not dead. You are not grieving for their death, you are grieving for your loss. But the more you indulge in self-pity, the worse you will feel. I am concerned not only for your emotional well-being, but for the effect it is having on your physical self. I can help you know what to do," I reminded him, "but only you can go home and do it."

"Oh, doc," Cody began, his drawl slower than ever, "you just can't understand how bad my situation feels. You'll just never know."

"You're right," I readily agreed. "In fact, I don't think I could ever really know how *anyone* else feels. What I do know is that you are feeling very sorry for yourself, instead of looking on all the good that has been given you. You've got a new kidney and a new chance at life. Instead of using that life for something important, you're wallowing in the muck about not having seen your family for awhile. I wouldn't argue it's a sad state, but I think you're making it worse than it is by not getting on with life."

"You just can't imagine," he continued as if I hadn't even spoken.

"Cody, I don't think *you* can imagine *what* I can imagine," I said. "Imagine a woman ten years younger than yourself, completely paralyzed from the neck down, in to see me for the nuisance of recurrent urinary tract infections. Her fiancé was killed at the time she was paralyzed, both of her parents are dead, all her caretakers are always people she meets anew and hires."

"Gee," Cody sounded more humble, "that's pretty awful."

"I thought it was fairly terrible. And that was the lady I saw right before I came in here. For as miserable as you feel right now, Cody, there are lots of people who are in far worse states who are moving on with life. You've got to move on, my friend. If you won't, there is no medicine and no magic that I know of that will help you." He seemed thoughtful, but not convinced.

When I saw him the following week, something was definitely different. He was teasing and joking at my office nurses in ways that seemed aggressive, with much sexual innuendos. When he teased me in a similar way, I laid my

feelings on the line. "Cody, I have always enjoyed our relationship, enjoyed our joking with each other. You know that.
But I will not tolerate this kind of joking. I don't find it
funny—I find it insulting. And furthermore, it's not really
you. I've known you for over a year now. You're a very spiritually inspired man. We've had discussions about God,
about Spirit, about the All of It, about the spiritual importance of the martial arts. What's going on here, Cody? What's
different today?" Something, I *knew,* was different.

"My internist put me on Prozac®," he said flatly. "It's a
medication that's supposed to help my depression. I've
been on it for two weeks."

"And do you feel less depressed?" I inquired.

"No, not yet," he said. "I feel about the same. My brother
told me that I seem to be acting different. He said pretty
much the same thing you did, but I just don't see it."

"Well," I offered him, "your personality is very different
on this medication. It is possible that the medication may
help you pull out of this slump. The medicine usually requires four to six weeks before the effects are really
noticeable. Since you've already been on it two weeks, I
would suggest you stay on it for at least another four weeks.
If it helps you in that period of time, then it's a good thing. If
it doesn't, Cody, you must do the reasonable thing and discontinue it. And you must know in the meantime that it has
changed your personality in a way that is not necessarily
more pleasant. I will continue working with you, but please
keep a check on your personality. If the drug takes away
your ability to do that, then I'm nervous about it. Let's see
what happens."

Several weeks later his depression was no better. He also
reported to me that I was not the only one to notice his personality change. "I don't think this drug is helping, and I
think maybe I should stop it," he announced.

"I agree," I told him. "If it's not helping you in the positive way and causing a deterioration in other ways, it is not of value to you. There's one other thing that must be considered, Cody. I know you know this, but just let me remind you. Any kind of drug may numb you and change your perception of your life. If this helps ease you through a transition, that may be desirable. The fact remains that the reality will still be there. These medicines don't make the problems go away. And they don't teach you how to deal with the problems. Even if the drug had helped, we would still have to bring you back to a comfortable life. The drug would have been a temporary solution if it had worked. It didn't, and now we're still left with the same set of problems. What do you want to do about this?"

I knew Cody needed some significant help getting on with life, but there had been no psychologist or psychiatrist who had really seemed to fill the bill. With an upcoming "Change Your Mind, Change Your Life" workshop, I felt Cody could be helped. He was very reluctant to attend a program with a group of sighted, "normal" people. With much coaxing and with an agreement that a friend of mine would pick him up, he finally decided to attend. What he found was a collection of lovely people, willing and waiting to help him. He found that there were other people to love and enjoy him and that he could love and enjoy others. *And* he found that it was important for him to get on with his life.

In the weeks that followed, his attitude was reborn. He had a new zest for life. He was entirely off all psychiatric medications and his other medications had been reduced to a minimum. His body was responding well to the renewed thought and decrease in medicines. All the while, our treatments of manipulation, homeopathy, acupuncture, diet, and herbs had been continuing. The program was intensive, but it seemed as if it was helping.

One day, nearly two years after I first met Cody, I had a

feeling that it was time to reevaluate. If the treatments that we were doing together were helping, we needed to know that so that we could continue. If they were *not* helping his physical circumstance, it would be important to know that, too. Evaluating his pulses, his spine, his lab work, and finally, looking in his eyes, gave me an inspiration. It was time to check again. Though I'm not an opthalmologist, it seemed to me as if something had changed within one of Cody's eyes. I sent him back to the original opthalmologist and her opinion was the same: "There's nothing I know to do, but let's have the retinologist look at him again." The retinologist examined him. His report was essentially unchanged. Cody was blind, and there was nothing that could be done about it. He would, however, refer Cody to yet another specialist. There was something, though he wasn't sure what, that seemed different in Cody's eye. Not being able to explain it, he decided to explore it.

The next specialist whom Cody consulted felt that there was a possibility of surgical improvement. Though it was a long shot, perhaps that huge cataract and blood clot could be surgically removed. There were no guarantees—he wasn't very hopeful. It could be done, however, and he was willing to attempt it. Cody, on the other hand, was not nearly as enthusiastic. The optic nerve in his other eye had been destroyed because of the surgery, not the diabetes. "What if they destroy this optic nerve?" he demanded of me. "Then there will be no hope of me regaining my sight."

"Cody, there's no hope now," I reminded him. "Once upon a time, no surgeon or opthalmologist would acknowledge that there was even a possibility of improvement. No one would touch you with a ten-foot pole in terms of surgery! We've worked long and hard for two years and now suddenly someone thinks there might possibly be some hope with surgery. I think the work we have done has caused that change. We've got to take it all the way. Who

knows how much longer it will take with our methods alone
to see more improvement? We might never bring your sight
back. If that cataract can be surgically removed, you might
be able to see again. You can't see out of that eye now, Cody.
I don't know what you have to lose."

"Aren't you holistic?" he snapped angrily. "I would think
you would want to keep using the herbs and acupuncture
and homeopathy."

"I *do* want to continue those things." I was almost pleading. "Cody, help can come from many directions. I am
interested in whatever direction provides that help. Remember that story I told you long ago? I don't care if we're
rescued by a boat or helicopter or the very hand of God
coming out of the clouds. I'm just looking for the rescue.
We've done our work with dedication for these past two
years. If we hadn't, we probably wouldn't be hearing from
the surgeon that something might be possible. Now that
something *is* possible, I say, let's go for it. What do we have
to lose?"

It seemed that Cody needed to think about this for some
time. After all, it was not just the disease, but the surgical
intervention that had caused his loss of sight in the other
eye. He was nervous about the treatment and justifiably so.
"Help can come from many directions," I reminded him.
"Maybe this is one of the directions that we are supposed to
combine with our other treatments." Finally, after several
weeks of contemplation, he agreed.

The eye surgery went smoothly. The cataract was successfully removed and the optic nerve was thought to be
intact. When the bandage was removed, Cody had a greater
sense of light and dark, though still no clear vision. Two
weeks after the surgery, he developed an eye infection. The
infection was severe and required a second surgery. "Now
what, doc?" he wanted to know. "Never give up," I responded.

After the second surgery, the eye began to heal. Cody began to heal—more in mind and body than I had ever seen before. It had been over a month since I had seen him due to the surgery and his recovery, and I was quite surprised when I walked into the treatment room. "A long, blue polka-dotted skirt," he announced—which is just what I happened to be wearing. "I was actually hoping for a miniskirt, doc," he grinned. I couldn't move. I felt temporarily paralyzed with joy. This man could see me! He stood up and moved closer. With his face barely two inches from mine, he said, "Doc, you're really pretty" and smiled.

"Cody, I've been trying to tell you that for two years," I said and smiled back. Then we both screamed, hollered, jumped up and down, embraced, hugged, cried, and hollered some more. Cody could see! He pulled out the picture of his daughters and showed it to me again. "Doc, I can see what they look like. They really *are* beautiful, aren't they? I don't drive yet, but I think I can. Every day my eye seems to be getting better. The surgeon is quite surprised. Said he's never seen anything like it before. I just don't think I can stop my treatments with you now. If you think I need to continue, we'd better keep doing what we've been doing. After all, no one thought there was any hope before we did these things together."

He once was blind, but now he sees. The words of the old hymn come back to me every time I think of Cody. His eyesight has improved dramatically and he is back in the land of the sighted. More important, he has picked up the pieces of his life and gone on to build a new life. Sometimes he sends patients to me. They tell me, "Do you know Cody? That guy who used to be blind but can see now?"

"Oh, yeah," I say with a grin. "Do I know Cody! Cody and I walked through the valley of the shadow of despondency and despair together. There were times when both his mental/emotional state and his physical state seemed desperate. Because he never gave up on himself, neither did I. Where there is life, there is hope—I believe that. Cody is the shining example of that."

It doesn't matter how much or how little we have. What matters is what we do with what we've got. Though Cody's wife and daughters have not come back, he is now able to talk to his daughters on the telephone. He assures them that he loves them and someday, I am confident, he will see them again. In the meantime, Cody has a life. Not just because he can see with his eyes, but because he can see with his inner knowing. The cure of his eyesight was a miracle, a combination of both conventional and complementary medicine. Hope and help can come from any direction. If you don't know that, talk to Cody.

13

AND A LITTLE
CHILD SHALL LEAD THEM

ammy was an energetic, adorable eleven year old with dark brown hair held in a high pony tail by a colored elastic band. Her smile and her exuberance were positively contagious as soon as she walked in the clinic. "Well," I said, "are you the patient? You look pretty great to me." She smiled and bounced in her chair.

"Yes, I'm the patient, Dr. Myatt," she announced confidently.

"Well," I told her, "I give up . . . tell me what's wrong."

"I'm hyperactive," she announced with all the boldness of a confident diagnostician.

"And how do you know this?" I asked her.

"I've been evaluated by school counselors *and* by two different doctors. I'm having trouble in school—my grades aren't very good. The teacher says that I don't apply myself, that I have too much energy."

"And is that true?" I asked. "How does it feel to you?"

"I guess I'm kind of bored with school," she told me. "Sometimes I don't pay attention. But sometimes I really try to pay attention and it just seems like I can't. I get in fights sometimes. I don't mean to. I don't exactly know how it happens. Anyway, it seems that I'm always in trouble at school. I'm in trouble a lot at home, too," she added reluctantly.

"Tell me what it's like at home," I questioned.

"Well," she said, "Mom is sick a lot. She asks me to do a lot of things for her."

"Like what?" I wanted to know.

"Well, like bring her a Coke® . . . bring her a candy bar . . . run to the store and buy cigarettes."

"How can you buy cigarettes for your mom?" I wanted to know.

"Oh, Mom writes a note and says it's O.K. The storekeeper knows that Mom is sick all the time and can't get out, so he sells the cigarettes to me."

"How do you feel about all of that?"

"Sometimes it makes me angry," she confessed.

"What about it makes you angry?"

"I don't get to play with kids. It seems that I'm always taking care of Mom. They taught me in school that smoking isn't good for you. But when I tell that to Mom and ask her to quit, she just gets mad at me. She says that with all the stress she's under, it's the only thing that calms her down. Sometimes we get in fights about it because I think she ought to quit smoking. Instead, I have to run to the store and buy cigarettes. I don't have time to play with anybody and sometimes that makes me sad."

Tammy seemed very mature for her age. The way she was discussing her condition with me indicated a degree of understanding beyond her years. Perhaps it was because of the adult responsibilities that had been placed on her. Though I kept the conversation light, I began talking to her in a more mature way. She seemed to appreciate it, and the communication between us improved.

"How long have things been like this?" I asked.

"Well, for about three years," she responded. "Everything was fine until I was eight years old. Then Mom and Dad got a divorce. After that, Mama stopped working. She's been sick ever since. Now we live with Grandma, who takes care of us. I like Grandma a lot, but she and Mama don't get along. They're always arguing and that makes me sad, too. Sometimes I wish Mama could just be like other moms. You know, go out, work in the daytime, and fix dinner. But she's not like other moms. She sits home all day and watches TV and makes me wait on her."

"I bet that's pretty tough," I said with true sympathy. She nodded silently.

"Speaking of dinner, I want to know what kind of things you eat. What do you usually have for breakfast?"

"Oh, you know, some kind of cereal. My favorites are Fruity Tooties and Sugar Crunch. At noontime I sometimes have the school lunch. Usually not, though. Mom says it's too expensive. I pack myself a lunch . . . peanut butter and jelly sandwich, a bag of potato chips, a Twinkie®."

"Does your mom or grandma ever fix lunch for you?"

"No, I fix it myself," this little woman-child responded.

"So then what do you do for dinner?"

"Sometimes Grandma cooks. Grandma fixes really good spaghetti. Sometimes Mom sends me down the street to the burger shop, and I get hamburgers for all of us. Otherwise, I just kind of get my own dinner—whatever's around."

"And what kind of things are around?"

"Oh, you know, sometimes I just snack. Maybe a Twinkie® or a fruit pie. Sometimes I get a hot-dog at the fast-food store down the street. Just snacks, you know."

"No, I don't really know until you tell me," I said with a smile.

"Yeah, I guess that's right," she agreed and grinned back.

"Since you're in town for one week for treatment, let's talk some more tomorrow. We may take a little blood test tomorrow, too. That will be O.K., won't it?"

"Will it hurt?" her voice was hesitant.

"Yeah, a little bit. Kind of like a big mosquito bite. Have you ever fallen off your bike and skinned your knee?" She nodded. "Well, I guarantee it won't hurt that much, and you made it through that O.K., right?"

"Yeah," she said. "I've had lots of skinned knees. If it doesn't hurt more than that, it'll be O.K."

"All right, I'll see you tomorrow. Have a good dream tonight and tell me about it next time I see you. O.K.?"

"O.K."

"Oh, by the way, I charge hugs for office visits. You can pay up now," I said and opened my arms wide.

She ran and threw herself against me like a little sponge, hungry for love. I hugged back. After what seemed like nearly a minute, I rocked her in a gesture that said, "Now it's time to go." A little part of me felt sad, as if I wanted her to stay so that I could hug her all afternoon.

The following day, I saw her mother as a patient. She had already received a diagnosis elsewhere. Her complaints included a stomach ulcer, irritable bowel syndrome, and general muscle aches and pains. She smoked cigarettes heavily, drank a lot of colas, and ate a very poor diet. In addition, she no longer worked or performed any type of service, but instead sat home watching television all day long. This, she claimed, was because she "hurt all over." She couldn't really work, she explained, because of her discomfort.

When I asked her why she thought she might have an

ulcer, she said it was because of worry. "And what kinds of things do you worry about?" I questioned.

"Well," she said, "I worry about not being able to support myself. I live with my mother and we don't get along very well, so that causes a lot of stress. And then, of course, I worry about Tammy. With all the trouble she's having in school, I'm just afraid for her and what her future might be. My life is really very stressful, you see."

"Did you know that the diet you're on, combined with the smoking, may have caused your ulcer? And did you also know that the type of diet you're on may be the cause of your intestinal troubles?"

"No," she said, she didn't know that. Further, she did not think that was possible. If it were, her medical doctor back home would have told her about it. Instead, she had been put on some anti-ulcer medication. Her doctor had mentioned once that she ought to quit smoking, but he never pressed the issue with her. Because of that, she didn't really think it was that important.

When I first started practicing medicine, I believed that patients came to see me when they wanted to get well. After being in practice for some years, I discovered that this is often, but not always, the case. Sometimes there are many reasons for a patient not to recover. It appeared to me that Tammy's mother, Eleanor, might be in such a category. The more she talked, the more I could see the "secondary gain" that she derived from being ill. Because of her complaints, her daughter felt responsible to wait on her. Also, by being ill, she felt excused from many of the responsibilities of life and of motherhood. Using her illness as the reason to be in a chair all day, she felt it acceptable not to take care of her daughter, not to cook, not to hold down a job. Her illnesses also were the reason that her mother had taken both her and Tammy in. After all, if Eleanor was sick and couldn't work, how could she care for a daughter? The illness had a lot of benefit to it. Though Eleanor, as with most patients, would not acknowledge this at first, it had to be considered as a possibility. In Eleanor's case, there was no aspect of her illness that was so debilitating that it would have prevented her from work, especially in the case of doing something meaningful and helpful around the house. Her illness did not, in truth, prevent her from "home work." It was enough of an excuse, however, both in her own mind and in the mind of her mother. It also seemed to be effective in manipulating her eleven year old.

Over the course of the next few days, I continued to have discussions with Eleanor. She had made up her mind to be ill, and there was no helping her change it. She informed me that she was sick and it was because life was stressful and there was nothing she could do about it. I tried to help her see how much good she could do in her own life if she would make some changes in her behavior, but she wouldn't hear of it. She was bound and determined to be sick. This, I believe, is anyone's right and anyone's privilege. For Tammy, however, her mother's choices were also affecting Tammy; the mother's choices were contributing to the illness of the daughter. There was only one thing to do as far as I could see. Toward the end of the week, I had a heart-to-heart talk with Tammy. If Mom would not change her behavior and help herself, it was up to Tammy to make her own changes. As with our previous visits, I spoke with her in a more adult tone, knowing she could understand it that way.

First, I explained to Tammy how her diet, which was high in sugar, could be contributing to or even *causing* her hyperactivity. Though I didn't go into all the biochemistry of the situation, I did point out that a young, rapidly growing body needs lots of nutrients to help it grow correctly. A diet that was mostly fast food and sugar did not contain enough of those important ingredients to help her grow up strong and healthy. I also explained how that excessive sugar could be overstimulating her nervous system, making it difficult for her to concentrate in spite of the fact that she was very bright. She seemed to understand and accept this. Then she asked the piercing question, "What do I do to make my diet better? It seems like it will be difficult with Mom the way she is."

I lowered my head and spoke in quieter tones. "Tammy, I've talked to your mom. I've explained some of these same things to her—how she could help herself *and you* by making some changes. It just doesn't seem to me like your mom is ready to listen or to understand at this time. Now, here's the challenge for you. Your mom is older. You look to her for the example and guidance. That's the way it usually goes with the older ones teaching the younger ones the proper way to live. In your mom's case, she's kind of forgotten, or maybe she never knew, some of these healthy principles. Right now, she's not setting the kind of example for you that will make you strong and healthy. You can wait for her to change, but who knows how long that will take. She might *never* change. She might always be the way she is. You're very mature; you can understand; you can do this, I know. One of your choices is that you make your changes *without* waiting for your mother or grandmother. I'll teach you what a good diet would be like. I'll help you to know how you can fix things for yourself, even good lunches to take to school. But if you're waiting for somebody else to fix you or give you these things, it might never happen. You are too intelligent to do poorly in school just because you're not able to concentrate. I believe that if you make some of these changes, you can help yourself get healthy."

"What will happen to Mother?" she asked. "How can I change her? I try to talk to her about the smoking. I try to ask her to fix us some regular meals, but it doesn't seem to make any difference to her. What about that?" she wanted to know.

"Yes, I've tried speaking to her, too, and she didn't hear me either. Tammy, I want you to just go ahead and do the good things for yourself. I know it's going to be hard sometimes. Your mother asks you to go get cigarettes, and you don't have time to play with friends. And it doesn't feel good to buy her cigarettes when you know they're not healthy for her. Maybe sometime you'll be brave enough to just say, 'No, Mother, I don't want to get your cigarettes and I won't. I believe that they're hurting you. I believe that if I go get them for you, then I'm helping you to hurt yourself and I love you. I don't want to do that any more.' It would take a lot of courage, but I bet you've got that much courage."

She looked thoughtful and then nodded. "Yes, I think I do," she said hesitantly.

"Tammy, you can't change your mother. You can only change yourself. Some of the things that I am suggesting that you do, like make your own lunches and fix healthier foods, are very grown-up things. Most kids your age would rely on their parents to do it for them. But you're not like most kids your age, and your circumstance is different from many other kids! You're going to have to be more grown-up and make more grown-up choices if you want to be well. When your mother sees you making healthy choices and if you'll stick to your guns, she may come around. She might change her mind and ask you what you're doing. Most younger people look to their parents for their example, for their model of how to behave. Your mom right now is not well, and she's not able to be a good model for you. Maybe you are going to have to be a model for her. At the very least, you can help *you* get well. And maybe, at the very most, you can help your mother recover as well. Tammy, it won't help your mother get well for you to be sick. Does this make sense?"

"Yes. Yes, it does," she said. I could almost hear her thinking.

Since Tammy was largely responsible for her own diet anyway, I taught her how to make healthier choices. We discussed the fact that she should always have breakfast and something better than a candy bar. She liked fruit, and she already knew how to scramble herself an egg. An egg, a piece of toast, a bit of fruit—that would be a good breakfast, we decided—and she knew that she could do that. For lunch, the school cafeteria always had some good things that included a salad bar. The problem was that her mother didn't always give her the money to eat at the salad bar. "Tammy, why don't you tell your mother that you want to eat healthier foods so that you can get well and that it would be much easier for you to be able to take the school lunch every day? Tell her that if she would decrease her smoking, she could give you the money you need to buy school lunch. Maybe it's a little manipulative," I admitted, "but why don't you make her feel a little guilty? After all, she's spending money to smoke, and we both know that's not healthy for her. Why can't she give some of that money to you for your school lunch?"

"Yeah, I could do that," she said enthusiastically. I could tell she was eager to try our strategy.

"If it doesn't work and you can't find money for school lunch, take some vegetables with you instead of potato chips. See if you can have a tuna or cheese sandwich instead of just peanut butter and jelly. And a Twinkie® every day for dessert? Well, maybe just a couple of times a week, hmm? Raisins would also be good."

"Oh, yes, I like raisins," she said. "I think Mother would buy those for me if I asked."

"Good!" I encouraged. "We're almost there."

Finally, we talked about dinner. "Tammy, your grandma knows how to cook, right?"

"Yes, and sometimes she does," Tammy offered.

"Well, why don't you ask Grandma to cook more often?

Tell her that you want to learn how to cook and ask her if she'd teach you. Maybe grandma would be a little more en- thusiastic about cooking if you asked her personally to do it. Have you ever tried that before?"

"No," she said, "I haven't. I bet Grandma would like to teach me how to cook."

"And while you're at it, why don't you tell Grandma that Dr. Myatt suggested you eat more vegetables? Ask her if you could cook some vegetables along with dinner. Do you think she'd do that?"

"Oh, yes," Tammy said. "Grandma knows how to cook vegetables. She pretty much stopped because Mom says she hates vegetables. But I bet if I told Grandma I liked veg- etables, she'd start cooking them again."

"Excellent." I could tell that Tammy had the strength and the courage to make the necessary changes. It was asking a lot of an eleven year old, but what else was there to do?

"Now what do I do when Mom is sitting home all day, watching the television and smoking and being sick?" It seemed like the final important question for which Tammy needed an answer. "When I come home from school and see her sitting there like that, I get so angry," she told me, but her voice didn't sound like the emotion of anger.

"How else does it make you feel?" I wanted to know.

"Well, I worry about Mom, Dr. Myatt. It seems like she's always sick."

"Tammy," I told her, "we've already talked about some very grown-up things, haven't we?" She nodded. "This is a really big, grown-up thing that you have to know. Your mom is sick and much of the reason she's sick is because of her own choices. You recognize that and that's why you get an- gry. You see her being sick and making herself sick, and I know that must be really hard for you to take."

"Oh, yes, yes, that's it," she said. "It really makes me mad and it makes me worried."

"Anybody can feel that way about anybody else. The fact that you feel worried is because you care about your mom. You've tried talking to your mom and so have I. And before you both leave, I'm going to talk to your mom again and help her know what things she could do to make herself healthy. You and I both know that she might listen, but she might not. If you let yourself continue to worry about your mom, then you're making *yourself* sick. Now I'm sorry and so are you that your mom is choosing to be sick, but it doesn't help her feel better for you to make yourself sick. Do you understand?"

"Yes," she said with a voice so confident I was convinced she did. "Mama's making choices that make her sick, and I worry about her because of the things she does. But my worrying about her won't help make her better, and it's also making me sick. I guess, in a way, I'm kind of doing what Mama's doing, aren't I?"

"How do you mean?" I asked.

"Well, I've been doing some things to make myself sick, too, haven't I?"

"Yes," I acknowledged, "and I think it's just because you didn't know. Now that you know, I'm expecting big things from you, Tammy. I'm expecting you to help yourself get well. And maybe, just maybe, your Mama might learn something from you. It usually doesn't work so much this way, but you are going to have to be the teacher to your mother, instead of the other way around."

"I understand," she nodded.

I saw Eleanor later that same day before they left. I reviewed with her all of the difficulties that I thought were contributing to her illnesses. I helped her know what dietary and life-style changes she could use to make herself feel better. The castor oil pack, I assured her, would be easy enough to do while she was watching her television and would greatly help her irritable bowel. Discontinuing smoking and making some dietary changes would almost surely cure her ulcer. I also mentioned how much her smoking was causing Tammy to worry. If not for herself, perhaps she would want to consider making some positive changes for her daughter.

She listened silently to everything I had to say, but there was no response. Finally, she began telling me all the reasons why she would not be able to do any of the things I had suggested. Her life was stressful, she was out of a job, she was too sick to work, and on and on and on. I wondered if all of my research on her behalf had been in vain. Nevertheless, I know that sometimes a seed has to be planted long before it finally sprouts. "Maybe some day when you decide you want to make some changes, you'll appreciate having these suggestions written down," I told her. And so I gave her a list of each of the items I had suggested with instructions. "Also, don't be surprised if Tammy does some things differently," I counseled. "She wants to make healthy changes in her life, and I'm certain she's going to do it. I hope you'll encourage and support what she wants to do. I believe that she can overcome her hyperactivity and start doing well in school. You know, some of her distress is really over worrying about you."

"Worrying about me?" Eleanor sounded incredulous.

"Of course. She loves you," I told her. "Don't you think that she worries about your health and welfare?"

"No," Eleanor said, "she's only eleven years old."

"What do you mean, she's only eleven years old? She's very mature for her age, partly because you have required so much responsible behavior from her and partly because she hasn't had the opportunity to be a normal eleven year old with friends and relationships. She feels that she has to take care of you and fuss over you so much that she doesn't have friends. Maybe, just let her be a child for awhile . . . let her be eleven. You also have to understand that she's very

mature and everything you do is influencing her greatly."
Eleanor seemed thoughtful, but not necessarily convinced.

The family left and went back to their home state. Two
months later I got a note from Tammy that said:

> *Dear Dr. Myatt,*
> *I have been doing the things that you told me to do. I*
> *am doing much better in school. Last report card I got*
> *three A's. I have been eating a good diet, and Grandma*
> *cooks more often now. I have vegetables every single day.*
> *One time Mama asked me to go to the store and get ciga-*
> *rettes, and I just told her no, and then I asked her if I*
> *could have the money for my lunch. At first I thought*
> *she was going to get mad, but then she said yes. Now I*
> *have lunch money every day and always eat a salad at*
> *school.*
> *Mama's trying to quit smoking. I think she really*
> *means it. She hasn't asked me to go to the store nearly as*
> *much. Maybe she will get better, too. Thank you for all*
> *the help. I love you.*
>
> *Tammy*

It was less than a week after Tammy's letter arrived that I
got a telephone call from Eleanor. "Well, Dr. Myatt, things
have been really different here since we saw you."

"Oh," I sounded as if I hadn't heard. "Tell me about it."

"Tammy has gone from doing poorly in school to being
one of the top students. Her teachers just can't believe how
well she's doing and how much she's changed. She gets up
every morning and cooks her own breakfast and helps cook
dinner every night. And she told me that she was sorry I was
sick, but that she wasn't going to make herself sick along
with me. That really shook me up. I just couldn't believe she
said that. And all of a sudden I realized I have an eleven-
year-old daughter who's been able to make changes in her

life. And here I am, almost forty, and now I'm learning from her. I changed my diet, too. Not as much as I could and not as much as you told me about, but quite a bit better. I don't sit and drink colas all day, and I don't eat much in the way of sweets. I've also cut my smoking just about in half. And you know what? I don't have an ulcer any more," she sounded triumphant. "My bowels have been much better, too. Tammy said she'd help me do a castor oil pack, so I've been doing them for a few weeks. They really do seem to help. Now I realize that I have to do something to get out of the house. I think I'm going to go back to work. I feel much better, and mostly I think it's because of Tammy's help. I think Tammy's better because of what she learned from you. Whatever you said to her, it really worked. I don't know how we can thank you enough."

"You don't have to thank me. Your getting better and Tammy's getting better is thanks enough. You've got a remarkable little girl there," I reminded her. "She's done an amazing thing for herself, for you, and for all of us."

"Yes, you're right," she said. "I just didn't see it before. And I didn't realize how much my illness was contributing to *her* illness. Thank you again. We'll be in touch."

Six months later I received a full report, including a photocopy of Tammy's report card. Seven A's, one B—the top student in her sixth-grade class. The school counselor was writing to me to find out what my treatment protocol was. I explained to her that it was really what Tammy had done and how she'd gone about it.

Tammy drops me post cards to let me know how well she's doing. Her handwriting and her vocabulary are quite advanced. And Eleanor . . . she's gone back to work full time. She has, to use the current vernacular, "gotten a life." So has her daughter.

The Bible says, "and a little child shall lead them." (Isaiah 11:6) Tammy showed all of us what that meant.

14

GRANNY

The old woman's name was Annabelle, but everyone knew her simply as "Granny." The grandmother of one of my closest friends, she seemed like kin to me as well. At age eighty-eight, she was as mentally alert as a thirty year old. She'd always been quite physically alert, too, except for some small difficulty with her eyes. On the several occasions that I had been with Granny, I had always heard her say that she was going to live to be a hundred. "Probably older," she said, "but at least one hundred." On her hundredth birthday, we planned to have a big birthday. She also knew that she would receive a birthday card from the U.S. president if she made triple digits with her age. Granny's philosophy of life had always been upbeat and optimistic. Even in the worst of times, she was able to find some good. When I asked her one day how she had managed to stay so youthful, she told me that it was because of her mental attitude. "When things change, I learn to change, too," she told me. It must have been so, because anyone of any age could sit and talk to Granny comfortably. Though she had seen the world go from horse-and-buggy to the Space Age, she remained flexible and vibrant. I had no doubt that Granny would live to be a hundred.

One day the phone rang, and I was pleasantly surprised to hear Granny on the line. This day, however, her voice sounded different—despairing. "How are you today, Granny?" I asked cheerfully.

"Well, I'm O.K.," she said. It was the closest I had ever heard her come to a complaint. "I'm not sure I want to live to be a hundred any more, though," she told me.

There was a long silence as I contemplated what to say. "Why, Granny, what's the matter?" I was shocked at her words.

"Well," she said, "it's this knee of mine. It hurts so bad, I can't even get up out of the chair. Why, I have to have someone help me out of the chair just to go to the bathroom! I can't even answer my own front door any more. If I have to be in this kind of pain until I die, I don't think I want to be a hundred."

"Granny, I never heard anything about this before," I reminded her. "When did this start?" I knew it must have been a problem for quite a while because Granny would not have been driven to despair so easily.

"Well," she said slowly and began to tell the story. "It first started over a year ago. I woke up one morning, and my knee was so swollen and painful I could hardly get out of bed. I went to the beauty parlor that day and had my hair done, and my daughter-in-law brought me home. She dropped me off outside at the driveway and by the time I had made it to the kitchen door, my knee was so painful I could hardly walk. I had to crawl across the floor just to make it to the telephone," she recounted. Calling relatives for help, she was taken to the doctor for a diagnosis. When the fluid was removed from her knee, her condition was quickly diagnosed as gout. She had never had an attack of gout before, and this seemed to the doctors as if it would be easy to treat.

Week followed long and painful week as each medication used for gout was tried in succession. Granny did not seem to respond to any of the usual medications. When the last drug was tried and had failed, Granny was admitted to the hospital for more testing. Recently, she told me, she had just been released from the university hospital in her home town. This particular hospital was one with a very high reputation, and they had performed diagnostic tests on Granny for two weeks before releasing her. What they had finally found was essentially nothing. The original diagnosis was found to be correct and, except for some cataracts on her eyes, she was in otherwise very good health.

On the day of her release from the hospital, her physicians had given her their final opinion. She was very old, what could she expect, really, from her physical condition? Perhaps the reason she was not improving with treatment was because of her mental attitude, they suggested. They told Granny that she was depressed and advised her to go on antidepressant medications. "Of course, I'm depressed," she scolded them severely, "and you would be, too, if you couldn't walk because of the pain in your knee!" Angry that their testing had revealed nothing and that their suggestion was one of antidepressant medication, Granny was discharged to her own home. Her physical condition was no better, and her attitude was certainly one of despair.

"Look, Granny, I have an idea. Right now I'm at a good place with my work. I could take a month off. Let me come back and live with you for that period of time so that we can reverse this condition. I know you can be helped, but I don't know of anyone in your area to refer you to. I think you'd be more comfortable in your own home, so why don't you let me come to you?"

"I know you're a good doctor," Granny said, "but I've already been examined by the best doctors in this state. If they say there's nothing that can be done, what makes you think you can help?" Her question was certainly legitimate.

"Well," I inquired, "what kind of a diet did they put you on through all of this?"

"They haven't put me on any special diet," Granny remarked. "And I wondered about that. Doesn't diet have something to do with gout?"

"Yes, Granny, it has a lot to do with gout. You know that and I know that, so there's at least one therapy that hasn't been tried yet."

"I asked the doctor if diet didn't have something to do with gout, and he said, 'Yes, but it wasn't important.' The drugs that they gave me should have done the trick. He said that a special diet was no longer necessary since these drugs had been invented."

"Granny, just say yes and I'll be there. I predict that it will only take about four weeks to straighten this thing out. Besides, it will be a vacation for me."

"Oh, no," she declined, but her voice was insincere. "I could never ask you to do something like that."

"Don't you believe that the things I will teach you might work?" I asked.

"Oh, yes, I do," she said, "but I just could never ask you to make that kind of sacrifice for me."

"You didn't ask me to make that sacrifice for you," I reminded her. "I love you; it would be my pleasure to do this for you. Besides, I've never been to anyone's one hundredth birthday party. I've been looking forward to it. And just think," I added, "when you recover and live to be a hundred, you can tell people who your doctor was!"

Although Granny was reluctant to ask me to make such a "sacrifice" for her, I also knew that her will to live was strong. I was frustrated for her to have this one, isolated circumstance of pain rob her of the joy of life. She must have felt this, too, because she was able to overcome her reluctance and agreed to have me stay with her for a few weeks and do what I could.

Granny was a lovely Southern lady. Her home was a huge, white plantation-style mansion with pillars on the front porch and a sweeping front yard. In typical Southern style, Granny had always had a gardener, a housekeeper, and a cook. Also, in typical Southern style, she had always enjoyed the fried foods and greens cooked with ham hock. In fact, her lifelong diet had been rich in fats. This had obviously never been a problem to her until recently. Coming from long-lived family lineage, Granny had survived and even thrived on what is today considered a high-fat diet. I knew that making some dietary changes would be one of the first orders of business.

When I arrived, I mentioned this to Granny. "Remember when you asked me if diet didn't have something to do with gout?" I questioned her. "Oh, yes, I'd always heard that," Granny answered.

"Well," I said, "it's entirely true. I think that making some diet changes will help your healing process go faster. I also know you've eaten this way for a very long time. Would you mind if we let the cook go on vacation for a few weeks until you get better? Then when she returns, we can show her what the new diet is." Granny agreed without hesitation. "I'll do whatever it takes," she said, "to get better."

Next, I looked at the night table beside her bed. It was covered with bottles of medication—prescription and non-prescription. There was aspirin and a second anti-inflammatory for the pain in her knee. There was something to help her sleep. There were all of the drugs that had been tried for her gouty arthritis, which was the diagnosis of her knee pain. There were several heart medications, only one of which I thought she needed. And there were various other remedies for runny nose, sinusitis, itchy ears. Except for the one heart medicine, which I determined she still required, I scooped the rest of the bottles into the garbage can. There was nothing in her collection that she needed to be weaned from, and I knew it was safe for her to suddenly discontinue these medications. *[Note: Do not discontinue any prescription medications without the advice and recommendation of your physician.]* Granny, it seemed to me, was greatly overmedicated. A large combination of drugs can act as a burden to the system. Many of the drugs, both prescription and over-the-counter, are toxic to the system, especially to the liver and kidneys. In Granny's case, good liver and kidney function was essential to her recovery. Any medication that we could do without, particularly by correcting the underlying problem, we would. I explained this to Granny, and she accepted my advice without hesitation. Not out of blind faith, mind you, but out of a deep desire to be well.

When I examined Granny, I found that her right knee was nearly three times the size of the left knee—swollen with what is known as gouty arthritis. The skin was red and very sensitive to the touch. Before the onset of the illness, Granny used to be quite active. Now, the pain prevented her from doing anything except sleeping and sitting in her chair. Her lack of activity further decreased the circulation which, in my opinion, was contributing to the problem. This difficulty is another "catch-22" for many people.

I explained it to Granny: "Whenever we have a condition that causes pain, our tendency is to stop moving because of the pain. In at least half of the circumstances that cause pain, good circulation is of utmost importance in restoring health. The problem is, the less we move, the less circulation we have. And so we have a vicious circle. The pain causes us not to move . . . the lack of movement decreases circulation, which causes further pain. This process can go on and on until we are entirely *unable* to move. The only way to correct this cycle is to create better circulation in the area."

Walking or leg exercises would certainly help, but Granny's disease was too far advanced for that. Even the slightest movement or contraction of the muscles caused her pain. As an alternative, I suggested that we begin with daily massage. Every day and sometimes twice a day, I would give Granny a massage. Although I would pay special attention to her knee, I felt that a full-body massage was essential. Granny had no trouble accepting this idea!

Edgar Cayce suggested in the readings that hot Epsom salt packs were helpful for pulling fluid from inflamed tissue. He also said that peanut oil massage would prevent and assist in overcoming arthritis. Every evening before her bedtime, we would do a hot Epsom salt pack to her knee, followed by a peanut oil massage. After each treatment, we could see the amount of fluid in the knee decreasing.

After a week of using the salt packs and massage, her knee was well enough to begin other treatments.

The other thing that Granny needed was exercise. After a long year of being in pain, she was disinclined to move. When circulation decreases, the problem increases. In other words, the worse it gets . . . the worse it gets. Exercise, combined with the massage that we were already doing, was the only answer to restore normal circulation. It became apparent that it was an important ingredient in Granny's cure. It also became apparent that encouraging Granny to do the kind of exercise I had in mind would be a little like pulling a mule to a place he didn't want to go!

Granny was a Southern belle to the core. At that point in time, I don't think she even owned a pair of pants. When I suggested to her that we buy her a sweat suit to make the walking easier, her face showed how appalled she was. "I don't wear pants," she announced definitively.

"Well, I know you haven't before," I humbly offered, "but we have a special circumstance here. Walking is going to be very important to restoring your good health. I mean *serious* walking. I'm not sure that your lovely wardrobe of dresses will be suitable attire for the task."

"But what if one of my friends sees me in a sweat suit? I'd be so embarrassed."

"Granny," I reminded her, "why would you need to be embarrassed about being athletic, about taking care of yourself?" I demanded to know. "Besides, I thought we'd go for walks down by the river. I really doubt that any of your friends will see us there." We stared at each other for a long time. "Granny, I really think this will help you." I could almost hear her thinking process. Finally, she said, "All right, you're right. Whatever you say. I do want to get better, and I know this is silly. You'll just have to put up with some of these attitudes of an old lady. But I can change; I'm willing to learn."

"Then I know you'll get better, Granny." I was triumphant.

We purchased Granny a pale blue sweat suit. I thought she was a beautiful sight to behold. She, on the other hand, was hoping that we wouldn't run into any other human beings on our walk.

We went down to a paved road by the river. Granny was very unsteady on her feet. Her knee still pained her. She walked with a cane, and we moved quite slowly. As we walked, we talked about important things. "Granny, all things considered, you're pretty young for a woman your age. What's been your secret to youth?" I questioned. This seemed like a good time for me to acquire valuable information about health and longevity.

"Well," she began, "it wasn't my diet. Being raised in the South, I've eaten all these fatty foods and fried things that you're teaching me about. Why, I never even ate vegetables that weren't cooked with a ham hock. I had a good husband and good children—that was nice." She tried to recount, but it was difficult.

"Well, what was your mind-set through all those years, Granny? It wasn't your diet, it wasn't necessarily what you were doing physically, it must've been something else—think."

"I guess I always just 'went with the flow,' " she said. "Yes, that was it. When things changed, I changed along with the circumstance. Yes, I believe that's it." She became more serious as she continued to speak. "You know, sometimes, when my friends need to sell their old house and move on or do something new, I hear them complaining about change. But why would they mind change—that's the nature of life. When it's time to move on, it's time to move on. I think I've always known that. I think I've always been pretty good at doing that. I guess maybe that's one of my secrets, if you'd call it a secret."

"It *is* a secret, Granny. Though the handwriting's been on the wall for so long, most people never figure it out. I'd be willing to bet that your flexible attitude, your willingness to change and to move and to grow along with life has helped to keep you young and healthy. In fact, it must've been that or something like it that's allowed you to feel so well in spite of some adverse physical habits. Of course, our attitudes are probably even more important than our physical habits. The handwriting's been on the wall a long time about that one, too, but most people haven't paid attention.

"It says in the Bible, 'As a man thinketh in his heart, so is he.' (Proverbs 23:7) That sounds to me like our thoughts and attitudes are relevant to us—probably including our physical selves, don't you think?"

Granny smiled. She was a devout Presbyterian, and I knew she liked it when we related our conversations to words from the Bible.

As we walked and talked, I noticed Granny standing straighter and walking with greater ease. She was relying on her cane a little less and was not absorbed in her appearance in a sweat suit.

"Well, Granny, this has been a good walk for you today. We'd better turn around and not overdo our first time out."

"Yes, this has been lovely, hasn't it?" she smiled. "I haven't been down here to the riverside in a long time. Did you know they used to have a carnival here? Every year, we'd bring the children down to this very spot, and they'd go on all the carnival rides. It really has changed a lot, but it's still beautiful." That was pretty much what I thought of Granny. She had changed a lot from the youthful pictures I had seen of her, but she was still beautiful and still a pleasure to be around.

"You know, Granny, sometimes young people don't like to be around old people, and vice versa, and for some pretty good reasons. I think one of the reasons that some families don't like to visit their elderly is because the elderly can get crotchety and cantankerous. They get stuck in their ways. But you're not like that at all. Maybe that's why the family always wants to come and visit you and genuinely likes to spend time with you. No one comes to see you out of a sense of obligation. People come because they enjoy your company. I think that quality has kept you young. And I'm certain that quality will help you recover from this illness. In spite of the fact that you have eaten a particular way and dressed a particular way and done particular things for the last eighty-eight years, you're still willing to learn something new. If you weren't, there wouldn't be anything I could do for you. Because you're open to new possibilities, I know you'll recover."

"I certainly hope you're right," Granny sighed. "It would be so nice to be rid of this pain."

And so we worked for just over three weeks, following our treatments of massage, Epsom salt packs, diet, exercise, and talking about beautiful and inspired things. One morning, on the twenty-fourth day of treatment, I came downstairs and saw a most unusual sight. It was Granny walking back and forth in the living room without a cane, kicking her ailing leg out in front of her deliberately like a German soldier. "It's a miracle, it's a miracle," she cried when she saw me come through the door. "The pain is gone. It's *all* gone," she emphasized.

"Then why are you kicking your leg out like that?" I wanted to know.

"Because I just can't believe that there's no pain," she explained. "I'm testing it to see if it's real . . . and it is. I woke up this morning and all the pain was gone. Not even a twinge."

"Well, isn't that happy news," I said with a grin.

"No," said Granny, grabbing me. "It's better than happy news. It's a miracle. Thank you." She grabbed me and squeezed hard. "Let's go out to lunch today," she suggested. "And let's invite my lady friends from the bridge club. They just won't believe this, they just won't believe this," she said as she headed off to the bedroom to get dressed. Out to lunch we went, with four ladies all about Granny's age. Two of them walked with canes, one was in a wheelchair, and one was unassisted, but walked with difficulty. And then there was Granny. She hopped in the front seat with me with all the bounce of a teen-ager. She still had her cane with her, and she propped it next to us on the seat. The ladies all chattered their chat while I chauffeured. "Oh, I almost forgot," Granny said, digging through her purse. "We've got to go to the bank first so that I can get some money. Dana, would you stop here? I'll just go to the automatic teller." As I pulled into a spot, Granny jumped out of the car, grabbing her purse and her cane. She started to walk off, but returned after only a few steps. She tossed her cane in the front seat of the car with me.

"Why, Annabelle, why are you leaving your cane here?" one of the ladies in the back seat wanted to know.

"Oh, that old thing," Granny called to us as she walked off, "it slows me down." She brushed the air aside with her hand and headed into the bank.

The chatter in the back seat increased dramatically. "She'll hurt herself walking without a cane," one of the women offered.

"No, look at her go," the other one said. "What has she been doing? Dana? Dana?" I felt a tap on my shoulder from the back seat. "Annabelle said you were coming to live with her for a few weeks to help her with her knee. What have you done? Could you help me?" The chatter began again, excitedly. And so, I started to tell the story, and Granny was soon back in the front seat to help me out. She enthusiastically related her experience to her friends, and they listened with awe. "But I don't know if I could eat like that," one of the women offered. "And exercise in a sweat suit?" said one of the others. "Did you really do that?" Granny looked at me and winked.

This year, 1994, Granny celebrates her ninety-seventh birthday. People that love her will come from around the world to share this important event. Her eyes are difficult for her now and her glasses are quite thick. She still walks unassisted, and her mind is as sharp as ever. One thing that hasn't aged at all is her youthful willingness to learn new things. I believe it's the most important reason for Granny's longevity. I know for a fact it's the reason that so many people love and admire this dear woman. And I am also quite sure that Granny will live to celebrate her hundredth birthday and, yes, we will be expecting a card and a phone call from the President . . .

15

D.O.T.O.
(DON'T OVERLOOK THE OBVIOUS)

"You're my last hope," the young woman told me. I might've been inclined to make a joking comment, but the seriousness of her expression told me otherwise. About my age, Jenny seemed on the verge of tears as she described her symptoms.

"I have this problem," she told me. "It really doesn't sound like much. Maybe you'll tell me it's all in my head. That's what other doctors have finally told me. All I know is, it makes me miserable and no one seems to know how to help."

"If the problem is not in your head," I said, trying to add some lightness to the situation, "where *is* the difficulty? Please tell me about it."

"Well," she said, "it seems that I have some sort of chronic vaginitis. It's worse right before my menstrual cycle, but it's always present. My husband is a medical doctor, and I've been to almost every gynecologist and expert in the area. All that anyone can tell me is that I have a chronic yeast vaginitis. The problem is that the medications don't seem to help."

"What medications have you used so far?" I was poised to write in her chart. She began listing them for me. The list went on and on. Indeed, everything that is used in conventional medicine to treat vaginal infections had already been prescribed for this woman. "Gosh," I mused, examining the list, "you really *have* tried everything, haven't you?" She nodded somberly.

"I know you probably have told this story many times before," I said, "but I've never heard it. Please, tell me what your symptoms are and take it from the top." With a deep sigh, she began to relate her experience.

Ten years prior, when she was in her early twenties, she and her husband began to think about having a baby. After several years of trying to conceive, they finally consulted a fertility specialist. At that time, she had been having mild vaginal itching and discharge. The itching was never severe enough to cause her to seek treatment. Multiple fertility work-ups had revealed nothing. Both she and her husband were found to be fertile, and there was no diagnosable problem to explain the infertility. Various drugs were tried to stimulate production of eggs, and, thinking that it might help increase the likelihood of conception, she was given antibiotics for the low-level infection. Also she had taken various hormones and even immune-suppressing drugs in case there was an undiagnosed hormone imbalance or inflammation as the cause of the inability to conceive. The list of therapies that she had received over the course of the next five to six years was staggering. It appeared that everything reasonable and some things *unreasonable* had been tried. She had been treated for problems that, on the basis of lab tests and physical exams, she did not appear to have—"just in case" that was the cause.

Perhaps because she was a doctor's wife, every doctor she had consulted had tried very hard to be the hero. Some of the treatments *were* quite heroic, to be sure.

Dye had been injected into the Fallopian tubes (the tubes that carry the egg from the ovary to the uterus) to determine whether they were open in a normal way. They were. Next a small flexible probe was pushed through each Fallopian tube to double-check the results of the first test. Everything was normal. The list of exploratory procedures and treatments went on and on.

During this period of time, her vaginal infections became increasingly severe. Beginning about five years prior to the time I saw her, her genitals were always inflamed. There was no time of the month, she said, when she was not extremely sore. Normal activities, such as sports, gardening, or even walking were impossible for her due to the irritation. She was particularly sad about not gardening, since she loved it so. But with simple outdoor activities (weeding, planting seeds), she would become so inflamed that she could scarcely sit or walk. In addition to the many drug therapies that had been tried, she had attempted many of her own self-care treatments as well. Using a blow dryer after bath and shower to remove all excess moisture was something that seemed to give some relief. She had used douches with vinegar, acidophilus . . . you name it, she had tried it. Now, she said, she was both unable to conceive and in chronic misery from the condition. When she recited to me the list of gynecologists and fertility specialists whom she had consulted, I knew that she had, indeed, seen some of the best. I could still remember Dr. Jack, my medical mentor, telling me, "If it was easy, someone else would've figured it out." I had one confidence, a sort of "ace in the hole," that I had never discussed with Dr. Jack. Sometimes the obvious is overlooked because it *is* obvious. If it wasn't something complicated, perhaps the answer *was* obvious. That was worth considering, I thought, in Jenny's case.

When I asked to examine her, I received the first note of jocularity in her words. "Oh, sure," she said, "fine. You know, when I go to a party and it's all doctors, I really don't recognize them at the party. I kind of only know them if I see them framed by a V, like the position my thighs are in during a gynecological procedure." She grinned, and I could sense that she felt hopeful for the first time in a long time.

Her condition appeared to be every bit as dramatic as she had described. All of her female genitalia were red, raw, chafed-looking. I felt a little twinge of discomfort myself just examining her. After the evaluation, I gave her my highest thoughts of hope. Her condition was probably not something that was just local. After all, every treatment, both reasonable and unreasonable, had been used locally to cure her difficulty. In spite of the best that was known, she was still ailing. Now it appeared to me that we must look for a general or systemic cause of her complaint. Although the symptoms were manifesting in her female parts, perhaps the condition was actually one of a more general nature. With instructions for her to keep an accurate diet diary for five days, plus taking the indicated homeopathic remedy, I sent her home. Though she didn't seem convinced that her diet was in any way related, she agreed to the plan. Desperation is a great motivator, and she was inspired to try whatever I suggested.

Five days later, she was back. Her diet diary had been kept with great attention to detail. Nothing was particularly remarkable except that her diet was the standard American diet: SAD. Not ghastly, but not particularly health-promoting either. She had taken the homeopathic remedy as prescribed and did notice some lessening of symptoms. She was eager to hear what the next diagnostic step might be.

"After careful consideration of your case and after looking over all of your previous medical records—which, I might add, reads like *War and Peace*—I have a working hypothesis."

"Yeah, it is a pretty thick chart, isn't it?" she acknowledged noddingly.

"On the basis of the symptoms you have described to me, I want to rule out the possibility of a food sensitivity. Without going into great biochemical detail, let me explain it a little bit so that you'll understand why we need to do this exploration. If you are consistently eating something that your body is sensitive to, you will have a symptom someplace. Any organ or tissue of the body can be the 'target tissue' for a sensitivity reaction. In your case, because of all the fertility studies and medications, the female organs of your body may have actually been weakened. I believe that you may have a food sensitivity that is manifesting itself in your female genital tract. The genitals are the target tissue for the sensitivity. There are two tests I'd like to do to prove or disprove this theory. First, I suggest that we perform a stool analysis, looking for both the presence of undigested food particles and for anything that isn't supposed to be there. Any undigested food will tell us about the state of your digestive enzyme function. An underfunctioning digestion can cause these sensitivity reactions. Also, if you have any uninvited inhabitants in your intestinal tract, like a parasite or an overgrowth of yeast, we need to know about that as well. The stool test will give us all of that information at one time.

"Second, I recommend a test for increased intestinal permeability. If your gastrointestinal tract *does* have any of these problems I just mentioned, this second test will tell us if the toxins or inflammatory substances are actually being

absorbed back into your bloodstream where, as I mentioned earlier, they can cause a problem *any place.* Usually
the site of the problem will be in each individual's area of
personal weakness."

"Whatever it takes," she said, "let's just get on with it."

In just under two weeks, I had the results of her report on
my desk. The results showed that she had an overgrowth of
yeast in her intestinal tract. This would explain the chronic,
recurrent nature of the yeast vaginitis. The intestinal tract
was acting as a source of yeast to the female system. She
also had the presence of a parasite—an organism living in
her intestinal tract that was not supposed to be there. To
what extent this was contributing to her difficulty, I could
only surmise. Anything in the intestinal tract that is not supposed to be there is probably worth eliminating. We began
treatment, in this case, with diet, herbs, and castor oil packs
to correct the yeast overgrowth and eliminate the parasite.
Her symptoms improved by about fifty percent.

Our next step was to evaluate for the food sensitivities.
Although there are many different laboratory tests to check
for allergy, none is universally reliable. Each in its own way
gives a piece of information. The diagnosis cannot be based
on any single test and all of the tests combined together are
quite costly. Although I was sure she would be willing to
bear the burden of cost, there is an easier and even more
effective way to determine sensitivity reactions. I put her on
my version of a metabolic clearing diet. This is a program
that eliminates all of the most common food allergens and
substances that cause sensitivity reactions. I also used a
high-grade, hypoallergenic protein as a supplement to her
diet.

Unlike most patients, she did not complain about the re-
striction to her diet. Again, her dedication to her own
wellness was obvious. Within the two-week period of dietary change, her symptoms improved even more. Also

within this time, her husband decided it would be wise to consult with me for his difficulty with high blood pressure. He, too, went on the metabolic clearing diet and found that his blood pressure dropped to normal. When I saw them the following week in the office, I had not one, but two, very happy patients.

Our next step for both of them was to reintroduce foods, one at a time, to determine which might be causing problems. There were certain foods that would definitely reinitiate a reaction in Jenny. Within a few hours of eating certain foods, her itching would flare up. Since we added new foods one at a time, it was easy to tell which ones were causing an aggravation.

George found several foods that caused an elevation in blood pressure and was very curious to know the exact mechanism of this change. What a delight to be able to share and exchange knowledge with another physician from a different healing profession!

Jenny's symptoms were dramatically improved—eighty to ninety percent better, she reported. There were certain foods she found she could not eat. She told me, in a tone that was almost confessional, about a dinner party they had attended. She had been feeling quite well and ate something at the party that was not part of her diet. Within two hours, the burning and itching had returned to full-blown severity. There was one difference this time, however. Instead of panicking and being filled with fear-thoughts, she now felt confident. She knew what had caused the symptom and she knew that she could avoid it. She now recognized that she was in control of her symptoms and that they would subside. This was very different from the attitude that she had had before—that all of her symptoms were in somebody else's hands, somebody else prescribing the right medicine. When she discontinued the food that she was sensitive to, her symptoms resolved quickly.

We also found that her body was very acidic. The normal biochemical state of the human body is just slightly alkaline. Edgar Cayce mentioned this before it was recognized scientifically. Although there are some specific places in the body that are always normally acid, like the stomach and the vagina, most other places in the body are alkaline in their normal state. Edgar Cayce went so far as to say that a body in its normal acid-alkaline balance would not contract a virus. This information, although not placebo-controlled, double-blind studied, is consistent with much of what we know about viral illness. People do tend to contract viruses more readily when they are under stress of any kind—emotional or physical. Perhaps in this regard, Cayce again was well ahead of his time. At any rate, we found Jenny to be *highly* acidic in the genital area, instead of slightly acidic, as is normal. This was interesting because her symptoms would always be lessened *after intercourse*. Seminal fluid is slightly alkaline. Could that alkalinizing effect be producing a change in symptoms? I wondered. I suggested that she try a baking soda douche. We quickly discovered that with any flare-up of symptoms, an alkalinizing baking soda douche would quickly reverse the problem. Another piece of the puzzle appeared to be that Jenny's system was overall too acidic. Many Americans fall into this category when they are following the standard American diet.

On a subsequent visit, I entered the examining room and found Jenny positively glowing. Though our aim had not been weight loss, she had lost nearly twenty pounds on the program. Somewhat overweight to begin with, she definitely looked and felt better with the decrease in weight. The body tends to normalize itself when given the proper conditions. That normalization will often correct a weight problem without really trying. That was only one of the reasons she was so happy.

"You're glowing," I reflected to her.

"Yes, I know," she said back confidently. "Yesterday I was out working in my garden, the first time in a long time. It's so wonderful to be able to go out and pull weeds and plant seeds and come in and not suffer physically for it. So there I sat, working in my garden, and the air was just that perfect temperature. The clouds floating by so puffy and white, it all seemed like a post card. It seemed like a miracle for me to be there . . . it's been so long. I can't thank you enough. I can't tell how good it feels not to always have this nagging problem. Maybe this kind of a difficulty doesn't sound all that serious, but when you are so sore all the time, it really is a problem. I guess it'd be hard to know just how awful it is unless you experience it. And the worst part was," she went on, "that I thought maybe it was all in my head. Because none of the cures seemed to work, I thought that maybe I was making it up." She looked at me and paused.

"Well, I could see the tissue," I replied. "It was raw and irritated. And while people can make and create illnesses out of thoughts, it was necessary that we explore a physical cause. Now that you know what foods you're sensitive to, you can choose to simply avoid them. And if you ever *do* get a symptom, you know exactly what to do. Another important thing is that you know that you are in control. You don't have to wait until somebody else tells you what to take or do. You have learned tools that you can use yourself. In a sense, I guess you have your power back."

"Yes," she said, jumping out of her chair and running to hug me. "Yes, that's the other thing. I feel as though I have my power back. Before, I felt so helpless. Everybody else was trying to 'fix the doctor's wife' and it didn't work. I could tell they were working hard, they wanted to be the ones to find my cure. Every time those symptoms would come back I would be so fearful. I'd be thinking, 'Oh, no, here we go again.' There was hardly a time when I wasn't suffering. Now, it's very rare that I have symptoms and, when I do, I know exactly what I need to do to correct them. Not only have you helped me know how to cure my illness, you've helped me find how to have my power back.

"I hope your schedule isn't already booked. I'm sending lots of people to see you. Everyone wants to know what I've been doing. I think because I've lost all this weight. I didn't realize how uncomfortable I was with that extra weight until it went away. I feel so good on this program, I just want to stay on it forever. I prayed every day for an answer to this difficulty, Dr. Myatt. I believe that God has sent you. You were an answer to my prayer."

"Well," I said, quoting a famous hero of mine, Jesus the Christ, " 'It's not me who does the work; it's the Spirit within me. He doeth the work.' I'm just thrilled to be able to have participated in your healing process. Feel free to send your friends to see me. I'd be glad to help them, too."

Now, I have added to the wisdom of my favorite college professor, Dr. Jack. I *do* agree that if a patient has seen many other doctors and no cure can be found, it is probably not an easy case. The Myatt Addendum is this: Sometimes the answer is so obvious that it is overlooked. In that case, even though the answer is easy, we make it difficult. May all of us be continually protected from that mistake.

16

LEARNING SOMETHING NEW

Sometimes, being a holistic health practitioner is very challenging, especially in light of today's political climate. For medical doctors who wish to be holistic, the problems are twofold: (1) they are not trained in the complementary or holistic healing disciplines, and (2) their medical profession frowns upon deviation from the accepted norm. For naturopathic physicians, the problems are similar but different. While my own profession is supportive and, indeed, grounded in holistic treatments, political aggressiveness from other disciplines of medicine persist. I and my naturopathic colleagues must be vigilant to protect our right to be holistic. The bottom line is that *all* physicians from *any* discipline, who are practicing "whole-person medicine," must be watchful. It's a challenge that goes with the territory. Some days it feels O.K. and some days it's a struggle. On this particular day, I'm not sure what my thought was about the subject.

All of us in the office, a collection of M.D.s, an osteopathic physician, and myself, had received an update about a medical colleague of ours who was being persecuted for his holistic practices. The FDA reportedly had used some gestapo-like tactics to raid certain medical offices and health food stores to confiscate vitamins and nutritional supplements. How could a thing like this happen in a free society such as ours? And yet it was happening. The information and the update of the circumstance were there before us. It was with that knowledge that I went in to see my next patient.

The person awaiting me in the treatment room was a rotund and jovial man close to fifty years old. He seemed eager to tell me his story and to get a prescription. When I asked him to describe his difficulties, he related the following story:

A year earlier, he had been traveling in Mexico. He acquired a severe case of diarrhea that didn't stop after several days. When he got home, he received an antibiotic for treatment. The diarrhea stopped, but he had severe lower bowel gas with flatulence. He had also developed a severe case of upper G.I. gas and burping. At times, the gas on either end was quite painful. More antibiotics were tried. To date, he had had multiple courses of antibiotics to no avail. He had been worked up, he assured me, by many doctors. Nobody could find the cause of his distress, and it was starting to interfere with many aspects of his life. What could I do, if anything, for his condition?

The symptoms that he described to me sounded characteristic of an overgrowth of candida yeast in the intestinal tract. "There are other difficulties that could also cause these same symptoms," I explained to him.

"We will need to rule out a lack of hydrochloric acid or digestive enzymes, a parasite in the intestinal tract, or a dysfunction somewhere along the intestinal tract." He assured me that all of those conditions had already been ruled out.

"Didn't you see what I am from my chart?" he asked me.

I had to admit that I had not noticed. I opened his chart and looked under occupation. It said, "physician." "I'm a gastroenterologist," he announced flatly.

"No bull?" I said, laughing. "And you came to see me to find out what's wrong with your intestinal tract?" My delight was evident. "Don't worry, your secret is safe with me," I cajoled him.

"Oh, it doesn't matter," he said. "My colleagues all know that I'm desperate to find out what's wrong. I'm not ashamed to be seeing you," he said and sat back with a bit of a chuckle.

I made my list of what are called rule-outs. This means that I consider everything that could be causing the difficulty and then perform some test or in some way convince myself, one by one, that the problem is not that. If I cannot rule something out, then I must consider that it could be the cause. On the basis of the tests he described to me, I was able to rule out every consideration except an overgrowth of candida, a type of yeast, in his intestinal tract. No, that had not been ruled out, he assured me. "In conventional medicine, we don't really consider candida in the intestines to be a problem, since it's normally found there. I do seem to recall that the old doctors used to believe in that, though," he added thoughtfully.

"Yes, they did, and for good reason," I said. "That's because it is a real condition, and it's probably what is going on with you. Candida is a normal inhabitant of the intestinal tract, but an *excess* of candida can cause problems such as you describe. Let me go consider the best course of action momentarily, and I'll be back to make my recommendations."

I left the room hastily and ran to my desk. It's not my nature to be paranoid, but having heard about the difficulties that our holistic colleague was having in his practice made me a little nervous. Could this be a set-up? Perhaps somebody was posing as a physician to find out what I would do? The thought crossed my mind. I mentioned it to my colleagues. They, too, did not tend to be nervous about such things, but it seemed possible to them. We looked the name of this doctor up in our physician directory. His name was indeed listed and he was, as he claimed, a gastroenterologist. I sat at my desk contemplating the circumstances. My intuition told me that this man was authentic. He really *was* a gastroenterologist and he really *did* have gastric problems for which he could not find a solution. Feeling confident that this was the case, I went back to the treatment room to make my recommendations.

I advised him about the necessary course of treatment. I was so confident that his difficulty was caused by yeast that I suggested we begin treatment immediately, even before the test results were available. More for *his* confirmation than my own, I suggested that we do a stool evaluation to look for the presence of yeast. I scheduled the tests, then made my recommendations for his treatment. We would use capryllic acid, a derivative of castor oil, to kill some of the excess yeast. During this same time, we would replace the bacteria that are normally found in the intestines by taking a bacterial supplement called acidophilus. A special low-sugar diet and castor oil packs were also prescribed. Four weeks later he was back in my office for his recheck visit. His symptoms had entirely subsided, he told me. It was amazing to him how quickly he had improved once the correct diagnosis had been made. "Why do you suppose I got this illness?" he asked. "On what level do you mean?" I questioned him back. "If you're talking about the physical, I think you contracted this illness when you had multiple and repeat courses of antibiotics. Or are you referring to a more 'cosmic' level of understanding? I think you had to acquire this illness to find out how miserable it is and then be successfully treated so that you will recognize this as a genuine diagnosis and disease entity when you see it in your practice. I'll bet you've seen lots of patients in similar circumstances that thought they had candidiasis. Is that so?"

"Well," he confessed, "I *have* had people tell me that they read a book and they think they have the symptoms of candida. And, yes, I have assured quite a few people that there was no such thing."

"Well, from that perspective, I suspect that this was your learning experience. Now you can go back and practice gastroenterology and not miss this diagnosis when you see it."

"You can be sure," he told me, "that I won't miss it. It's very uncomfortable, and it deserves to be taken seriously. I thought I knew all the answers about gastroenterology, but this has certainly taught me something new."

"Being willing to learn something new has not only made you well, but it has made you a better doctor. Congratulations on both."

17

THE HEART OF THE PROBLEM

I reviewed the chart briefly before I entered the treatment room. My handwritten notations were apparent from the year before. Mary Jo—a short, rotund woman—had consulted me nearly one year earlier. She had had high blood pressure and a history of a small stroke ten years previously and wanted to know what preventive measures to take. Following my evaluation, I determined that she was at high risk for another stroke or heart disease and made the appropriate dietary, life-style, herbal, and homeopathic recommendations. Mary Jo had not come back for follow-up, and so I didn't know if she had followed the treatments or not. Now, nearly twelve months later, I would find out what had become of her.

It's a good thing I looked at the chart before I opened the door because I never would have recognized her. Though still pudgy, she was quite a bit slimmer than I had remembered her. Her skin was ashen-colored. She also looked quite frightened. Her appearance was alarming.

"Why, Mary Jo, it's good to see you again," I said enthusiastically, trying to elicit a smile from her. She remained very somber and said, "Yes, I'm back."

"Well, it's been quite some time since I last saw you," I pointed out. "Tell me how you've been in the last year."

"Well, quite a lot has happened since I saw you a year ago," she announced quietly. "After I saw you last, I went home and tried to follow the diet that you had give me. I was doing pretty well with it, but then my friends started to say that I was looking too skinny. When I'd go out to eat lunch with the members of my bridge club, they'd say, 'Aw, c'mon, Mary Jo, you can have just a little of this or a little of that.' I lost my resolve and wound up not following the diet you gave me at all. Then I was too embarrassed to come back to see you. Besides, I figured if I wasn't following your advice, what more could you do for me? So, things just went on. Two months ago, I started having chest pains. I came here to see you, but they told me you were on vacation. The pain got pretty bad, so I went to the hospital. At the hospital I was told that my coronary arteries were blocked and that I would need quadruple by-pass surgery. When I asked them if there was any other way we could treat it, the doctors told me no. They said I would have to have coronary by-pass surgery or I would surely die. So, two months ago that's what happened—quadruple by-pass surgery. My back and chest have been very painful ever since the surgery."

With that, she immediately unbuttoned her blouse and showed me the scar on her chest. All I could do was shake my head and say, "Wow." The scar ran from her throat down her entire chest and across part of her abdomen. It was very dramatic.

"I don't doubt that your back and chest hurt," I remarked. "When they do by-pass surgery, they pry the bones of your chest apart to access your heart. Just the bone and muscle trauma from that can cause a lot of residual pain. I know if we get you started with some massage and manipulation and possibly acupuncture, you'll feel much better. So, tell me what else is happening now."

"Well," she went on, "it seemed as if I was doing O.K. after the surgery. One of the doctors at the hospital, a fellow I really didn't like very much, told me that he hoped I lived quite close to the hospital. He said if I ever had chest pain again, it would probably be from a heart attack and that time would be of the essence. I have pain all the time in the front and back. I'm so afraid that I'll have a heart attack and I won't know it. I don't know if I should try to move so that I would live close to the hospital or not. What do you think?"

"Next time you have chest pain," I suggested, "come straight here to the clinic. We'll do an EKG right away. If the EKG is normal, then your pain is probably coming from the chest wall or spine, a result of the trauma of surgery. At least we'll know one way or the other when we need to be nervous and when we don't. Now there's something else that's very important," I went on. "We need to know the current level of your blood fats. Having by-pass surgery does not prevent you from having future difficulties."

She looked at me quizzically. "What do you mean?" she demanded. "I thought that the arteries had been fixed by the surgery." Her voice was quivering.

"Mary Jo," I said in a calming tone, "let's think about this for a minute. Atherosclerosis, which is what you had, is a blockage of the arteries in the body with fatty deposits. Those fatty deposits don't just block the arteries in the heart; they can build up in *all* of the arteries in the body. Any one of those arteries can lose a piece of that deposit. When that happens, it results in what we call a stroke. Also, if the high blood fats that originally caused the atherosclerosis are still present, the condition will reoccur. Didn't your surgeon discuss this with you before surgery?"

"No," she said. "I'm on a medication to lower my blood pressure, that's all. The doctor didn't say anything to me about diet."

I felt a sense of sadness at this report, but not surprise. Many of the illnesses that are treatable through diet are, nevertheless, *not* treated in this manner by conventional medicine. We are often so ingrained with the idea of using drugs and surgery that the simpler, gentler, and most effective treatments are sometimes overlooked. This is often the case in cardiovascular disease and it certainly was the case with Mary Jo.

"Well, there's one easy way to know what's happening," I said. "Let's take a measure of your cholesterol, triglycerides, and other blood fats today and repeat it in two weeks. That way we'll see if they're changing. If things look like they're becoming a problem, we'll have to take action. We may wind up doing the same things that we originally prescribed."

What I thought to myself, but didn't say to Mary Jo was that the original treatment that was prescribed would very likely have prevented the surgery. Now that she'd gone through this heroic treatment, she would probably still need to make the dietary changes to prevent recurrence. She was in enough pain that it didn't seem valuable to add to her distress by pointing this out, so I kept it to myself.

Her blood test revealed that she was in a high-risk category for coronary artery disease. This risk factor is calculated using the cholesterol level plus the number of high density lipoproteins (the good cholesterol). On the basis of this ratio, an accurate prediction can be made about the possibility of developing coronary artery disease. Though Mary Jo had just undergone quadruple coronary by-pass surgery, she was still in the high-risk zone. What this meant was that if we did not make changes, her new arteries could wind up being blocked just as the old ones were.

We repeated the lab work in only two weeks. This is a fairly short period of time to repeat this type of blood work, and I would not have expected it to change by much. The fact was, her coronary risk profile had elevated to the *highest* risk category. Mary Jo was at great risk for having another heart attack or stroke or both. This, in spite of the fact that she was only two months past surgery. The surgery alone might have had some effect, but it was not changing the course of her disease. Statistically speaking, coronary bypass surgery does not prolong life. The reason it is performed is reportedly to "improve the quality of life." Whether or not the surgery was necessary in her case would always be a question in my mind. There was no doubt about the circumstance now. Her risk for recurrence was very high and was escalating at an incredibly swift pace. Though I didn't want to alarm her, I felt it important that she understand the severity of her circumstance. I called her on the phone and suggested we have a visit very soon for a report of findings.

I explained all that I knew to Mary Jo. Her risk factor might have been lower right after the surgery, but it was escalating again at an alarming rate. We would be right back to "square one" if we didn't make some changes. The original diet that we had recommended was very important. In fact, studies have shown that coronary vascular disease can be reversed by the appropriate diet. In truth, this is probably much more effective than surgical correction because it can result in a reversal of deposits in *all* vessels in the body, not just the coronary arteries. Furthermore, it provides the long-term correction for the difficulty, not just a short-term "patch." Some surgeries that we perform today are lifesaving and wondrous procedures. Statistically speaking and on the basis of many patient outcomes that I have seen, I am not convinced that coronary by-pass surgery is one of them. There are much more effective and longer lasting ways to reverse coronary artery disease. In Mary Jo's case, it was too late to speculate about what might have been had she originally changed her diet when I recommended it. What *was* clear is that changes would need to be made now or she'd be right back where she was several months ago. I emphasized the urgency of making changes. Her blood fats and her coronary risk profile were deteriorating rapidly.

The fear of a reoccurrence increased Mary Jo's motivation to follow the diet. It had also become clear to her that the dramatic surgery that she had undergone was not curative. She was now ready to make the diet and life-style changes that would be helpful to her.

On several occasions when she had episodes of pain, the anxiety was virtually overwhelming. Several times, fearing a heart attack, she went to the emergency room. On one occasion, she waited six hours to be treated. She was told that her pain was not coming from her heart. After that, when she would experience pain, she'd come to my office where I would perform an EKG and read it. On every occasion, her EKG did not show her heart to be the cause of the pain. She finally became a little less fearful at every twinge and recognized that much of her pain was due to the trauma of surgery. With weekly massage, spinal manipulation, and acupuncture treatments, her symptoms subsided. The great fear that had been invoked in her at the time of surgery—her being told that any pain she had was probably a heart attack—did not help her condition. Now we had to treat not only the physical condition, but the extreme degree of fear that had developed surrounding it.

We started Mary Jo on a high-fiber, very low-fat diet. She followed it faithfully. Castor oil packs over the liver were recommended because they improve the way the body utilizes fat. The castor oil packs also helped to ease some of the residual muscle pain that she was experiencing and worked quite well in combination with massage. We used herbs, both to treat a slight case of constipation and to improve fat metabolism. Mary Jo lost her excess weight readily and, within two months, was down to a low, normal weight for her height and age. I warned her that as she came closer to a very desirable weight, she might hear discouraging things from friends and family. People around us tend to say things like, "Oh, you're looking so thin and pale," when we lose weight. Even if our weight loss is actually very healthy, for some reason friends and family often discourage us. I cautioned her not to listen to these scary stories, but to persist in her efforts.

In my professional opinion, she was looking healthier and moving herself toward a higher state of health. Though she did indeed encounter such disparaging remarks from those around her, she persisted in her own efforts and ignored what people were telling her. In fact, to one obese neighbor who commented on how skinny she was, Mary Jo boldly replied, "You're just jealous because I'm losing weight." This story made me laugh when she recited it because she actually was a very shy woman by nature. In taking control of her health and her life, she was discovering new-found strength that she had previously not known she had.

Mary Jo's EKGs, which are a picture of the electrical activity of the heart, were abnormal but stable following surgery. After a heart attack or an injury to an area of the heart muscle, the EKG will show that previous difficulty for a long time to come. In fact, in most instances, the EKG will remain abnormal indefinitely. As long as it remains stable, this does not reflect a problem. However, it is very rare and, therefore, not anticipated that an EKG will return to normal. I was not looking for or anticipating normalcy, only stability in her EKG tracings. By now I have learned to expect anything. Mary Jo was one of the first to teach me that.

Six months after her firm resolve to make the necessary changes, we repeated both Mary Jo's blood work and her EKG. The results were staggering. Her coronary risk profile (again a prediction of risk of coronary artery disease) now put Mary Jo in the *low risk group!* Her EKG was very close to being entirely normal. Her attitude and outlook were continually improving.

It took quite a bit of counseling, both in my office and with a psychologist, but the cause of Mary Jo's fears, both before the by-pass and after, were addressed. We had her old original fears to deal with as well as the new fears surrounding her risk of heart attack. When she came to recognize that fear was an emotion that could harm her heart, she began to learn new and more productive ways to face life.

I helped her know how to tell the difference between true cardiac pain that needed to be attended to and simple fear. That was not an easy task, but she was a willing student.

Another thing we noticed during this process was that her blood pressure was consistently lower. In fact, on one occasion, the symptoms that she described sounded like her blood pressure was *too* low. Examining her circumstance and her current medications, I suggested to her that we needed to wean her off the blood pressure drugs that her cardiologist had prescribed for her. I contacted her cardiologist to consult. "Dr. Smith, I am calling regarding our common patient, Mary Jo M. Have you noticed that her blood pressure has greatly decreased and is now actually below the normal range?" "No," he told me he hadn't noticed that. "Well," I said, "she's in my office today and her blood pressure is 90/60. Last time I saw her it was 120/70, and she was feeling fine. Today, at this blood pressure, she's having symptoms that suggest that her blood pressure may be too low. I think it will be helpful for her to be weaned off her blood pressure medication."

"Oh, no," Dr. Smith said. "Don't do anything with that.

She'll require the blood pressure medication for the rest of her life."

"Dr. Smith, it was not my intention to wean her off the medication that *you* prescribed. However, I think you need to reevaluate her circumstance in light of the many changes she's made. Were you aware that two months after surgery her coronary risk profile put her in the highest group and that currently she is in the low-risk group?" He replied that he was not.

"Further, did you notice that her blood pressure has gone from 180/90 to today's visit of 90/60? Have you seen her serial EKGs which show her electrical activity moving closer toward normal? In fact, if I did not know of her history of heart attack, it would not be evident from her current EKG. In my experience, this is a rare occurrence. Have you evaluated this information or are you aware of it?"

"Well, no," he said. "No, actually I haven't. Perhaps you could fax me that information."

"Yes, I'd be glad to."

"I just don't see how we can take her off her blood pressure medication," he went on. "I'm sure she'll require it for the rest of her life."

"Dr. Smith, surely you know that significant changes can be made in the cardiovascular system of people who change their diet and life style? Mary Jo has done that very thing. She is on an excellent diet and exercise routine, she's lost all of her excess weight, and she herself has created these changes that I'm describing to you. Though it may not be something you expect to see in your office, it is not only highly possible, but quite probable, if a patient is willing to make changes. Mary Jo has made these changes, and her blood pressure medication needs to be reevaluated."

"All right," he said. "Fax me the information and ask Mary Jo to schedule an appointment with me. This is very unusual, indeed, but I'll take a look at it."

I hung up the phone feeling somewhat disappointed about our conversation. Why was a doctor so reluctant to consider that a patient could actually get better and have a decreased need for a drug? Of course, I answered my own question. It is not part of the training or the philosophy in conventional medicine to study the effects of nutrition on disease. This is one area of conventional medical training that is both understudied and often underappreciated. Medical doctors actually often know very little about therapeutic diets, their effects, and how to prescribe them. It shouldn't have surprised me, I guess, but I was amazed anew.

I went back in to talk to Mary Jo. "You'll need to schedule your appointment with Dr. Smith. Though it wasn't an easy go, I think he understands the need to reevaluate your blood pressure medication. If he's not willing to work with you, I suggest we either find another cardiologist for you to work with or I'll wean you off the medication myself. It would really be my first choice to have you go in there and teach Dr. Smith something new that I don't think he knows yet. In fact, I predict he'll be swinging from the chandelier with excitement when he finds out what's really going on with you. In the meantime, keep up the good work and continue all of your therapies."

"Oh, I will," Mary Jo assured me confidently. "I know I have to do this to save my own life."

A few days later I received a phone call, not from Dr. Smith, but from Mary Jo. "Well, Dr. Smith agreed that I needed to be taken off my high blood pressure medication," she told me. "He wasn't very impressed by the changes in my blood work or my EKG, like you thought he'd be."

"What d'ya mean?" I was incredulous. "Didn't he think that was an amazing change? After all, this really was not an expected spontaneous remission. Not without the patients' heavy involvement in their own care and a major change of life style."

"No," she said, "he just looked at the numbers, shrugged his shoulders and said, 'Well, it does look like your blood pressure's too low . . . here's how to decrease your medication.' At the very end he asked me what I had been doing. When I told him about my therapies, he shrugged again and left the room."

"Well," I reassured her, "I have no explanation for his behavior. I really thought he'd be ecstatic to see such an improvement and to learn something new if he didn't already know it."

"I thought he would be, too," she said rather dejectedly. "You know, I never really liked that man. Do you think there's somebody else whom I could work with for my cardiologist?"

"Yes, I do," I said. "I have several excellent referrals, any one of whom I think you'd like, and I think we'd better send you to a new cardiologist. The heart not only relates to circulation, but it relates to our feeling of the emotion of love. I think it's important that you like and have good feelings about your cardiologist. If you don't, then let's find one whom you *do* feel that way about. Here's the name of a doctor. I'd like you to call her and schedule a visit. I'll call her first to let her know you're coming and to explain your situation."

When I called Dr. Nadell and told her about Mary Jo, she sounded positively thrilled. "It's not often that we see dramatic changes like that after by-pass surgery," she affirmed enthusiastically. "Sounds as if all I'll really be doing is monitoring her. It's probably wise for her to be seeing a cardiologist, just in case she has any future problems. Thank you for the referral, and I look forward to seeing her."

"Well, I know she'll look forward to seeing you, too. I think she'll have good feelings about you and, in my opinion, that's an important aspect of the doctor-patient relationship."

"Yes, and please send me those medical records," Dr. Nadell requested. "Again, that's a dramatic change. I can't wait to see her serial test results."

"I knew you'd be enthusiastic," I said. "We'll get them right to you."

Mary Jo and Dr. Nadell did indeed establish a good relationship. Mary Jo was much more comfortable and increasingly less anxious about her potential for future heart problems. She remained on her program of diet, exercise, relaxation, and herbal remedies. Several months later, her blood work showed that she was in the very lowest risk category for coronary artery disease. Her EKG had returned to an absolutely normal reading. Her risk for developing future problems, if she stays on this similar course, is much lower than the general public. In fact, her risk now for coronary artery disease is very low, even compared to those people who have never had a cardiovascular problem. She is off all medications, including her blood pressure medication. Her blood pressure remains low—normal. Most important, Mary Jo has regained a sense of herself and her own power. Before the by-pass surgery and for the two months after, she felt helpless. She was fearful, convinced that her life was hanging by a thin thread, held in someone else's hand. That fear was not helpful to her healing process and, in fact, was acting in a toxic manner toward her heart. As she has become more comfortable with her physicians and as she has recognized that most of the power is entirely within her control, her confidence has blossomed. Where once she felt helpless, she now feels powerful. She recognized, though perhaps through a difficult method, that her risk of cardiovascular disease largely resides with her. The choices that she makes on a daily basis, just as with all of us, are what will determine her fate. Now that she is "in the know," she is also "in the low"—risk category, that is.

I evaluate Mary Jo once a year for her annual physical

exam. She is the epitome of health and happiness. Except for the scar that she carries on her chest, there is no evidence on her physical exam that she has been through quadruple by-pass surgery. I wonder, did Dr. Smith think that her surgery had caused that change? If he did, he is deluded. It was Mary Jo who caused that change—through her own choices. Those same sets of choices are available to each and every one of us, when we find the courage and the strength to make them.

18

To Speak the Truth

In spite of her excess weight, the young woman in the treatment room looked frail and in pain. With one hand gripping her abdomen, she extended the other in a gesture of greeting as I entered the room.

"My name's Lisa," she announced to me, "and I'm here to see you about my tongue."

"Oh?" I said, somewhat surprised.

With her hand still gripping her abdomen, she sat, partially doubled over. I would have guessed from her appearance that her complaint was an abdominal one. Instead, she related to me the long story of her tongue problem.

For many years, it seems, she had had an especially sore tongue. It hurt most of the time and was particularly aggravated by certain foods. Though she had seen numerous doctors, no one had ever suggested what the problem was. "Geographic tongue," they called it, which is more of a descriptive term than a diagnosis. When I asked to see her tongue, it was, indeed, unusual. Deep fissures marked its surface. In our conventional way of thinking, there are a number of difficulties and deficiencies that could cause such a problem. I began to make my rule-out list as she continued speaking.

When I asked about any other health complaints she had, I was not surprised to hear that there was more to her story. She had had a history of an ulcer and now her abdominal symptoms felt like that again. It was difficult for her to sleep at night, and she had been given some medication for this. Frequent headaches and "just not feeling right" were a part of everyday life. When I asked about possible stresses in her life, she rolled her eyes and clenched more tightly to her abdomen.

There were circumstances both at work and at home that felt stressful to her. Part of the difficulty sounded easily correctable to me. It was not so much the stress of the circumstance, it seemed, but the coping mechanism she had learned to deal with those circumstances. When her boss would ask her to stay overtime, doing extra work for no money, she would always say yes when she felt like saying no. It wasn't that she was afraid for her job—she was not. Instead, it seemed more like something that she had learned over the course of many years. Nice girls don't say no, in effect. Whenever Mom, Dad, boss, roommates, or others asked her for something, she was always the "yes woman." As a result, she felt abused and taken for granted emotionally. When I reflected this back to her, she recognized it immediately.

"I'll need all of your old medical records," I told her. "I have a list of all the things that could be causing your difficulty. One way or another, we have to be able to rule out each of the items on my list. Some of the things, like an iron deficiency or a B-vitamin deficiency, have probably already been looked at. When I get your medical records, I'll see what tests have been done and what tests might still need to be done. I'm sure, with so many other doctors looking at you, that many of the things on my list have already been explored. Also, I'd like you to keep a diet diary for me. Write down everything you eat and drink for three days. Next to that, make a note of any times that your symptoms seem worse. Not just your tongue symptoms, mind you, but your sleep difficulties, stomach troubles, headaches, the works. We'll see if there's any connection to anything you're eating and some of the complaints you're having. From the Chinese perspective of the body, the tongue is simply an extension of the stomach. No Chinese physician would be surprised that you're having both stomach pains and tongue discomfort. If we can't find the answer through our Western way of thinking, we may need to consider some of these other perspectives as well." With what looked to me to be a renewed glimmer of hope, she took the paper from my hand with all of her instructions written on it and we said our good-bys. We would see each other again and re-view notes in a week.

As I suspected, her medical records ruled out many of the possible causes of her tongue complaint. In fact, it appeared to me that all of the Western diagnoses for this condition had already been looked at. "How frustrated she must've been," I thought to myself, "to have consulted so many doctors, including specialists, only to be told that essentially there was nothing wrong and there was nothing to be done." That difficulty, I know, is one that is faced by a number of patients.

Lisa returned the following week with her diet and symp-tom diary in hand. She had been very faithful in her record-keeping, usually an indication of someone who really wants to get better. We reviewed her diet history together and found some things that could be contributing to her problem. I pointed them out to her. "There's lots of fast food and processed foods in your diet, Lisa," I pointed to the diary. "It also looks like your stomach pain is worse every time you eat something that has wheat in it."

"My brother has Crohn's disease," she said, as if suddenly remembering. "Does that run in families?"

"It can. A sensitivity to something that you're eating could also be in your family. Let's make some changes in your diet for a while and see if that makes the symptoms better." She readily agreed.

Once Lisa began a wheat-free, sugar-free diet, her symptoms improved dramatically. The stomach pain that had bothered her was essentially gone. Next, we added herbs and castor oil packs to improve liver function. Although her liver function tests (blood tests related to the liver) were normal, we still had reason to believe, on the basis of her symptoms, that her liver might be in some distress. At this point, I explained to her that we were now considering her symptoms from a Chinese perspective. "Different systems of medicine look at the body in different ways," I explained. "When we run out of answers from one way of thinking, we try another way of thinking. Very often, that's how we come up with a solution."

Lisa didn't seem to care where the answers came from, as long as they continued. Castor oil packs for the liver, some spinal manipulation, and acupuncture all contributed to her treatment plan.

Lisa's physical symptoms were better, and she was responding well to treatment. Although her tongue still bothered her, all of her other symptoms were lessened to some degree. Except perhaps one thing, which I was quick to point out to her. All of her difficulties—stomach pain, headache, sleep disturbance—would flare up whenever she was working overtime. When I questioned her about it, we were back to the same old story. It wasn't so much the overtime that seemed a problem to her. Instead, it was more related to the frustration, the inability to say no when she really *felt* like saying no. "Lisa, if you feel as if you're being taken advantage of, you have to learn to say no. If you don't know how to do that, just watch TV. They've got some real good ads that teach you how to 'just say no.' " Though we made a joke out of it and laughed, Lisa knew that it was true.

"Well," she said after several minutes of thought, "I guess I don't have anything to lose, do I?"

"What do you mean?"

"If I tell my boss, 'No, I won't work overtime,' he will either say O.K., in which case I'll feel better, or he'll fire me. If he fires me, I'll need to find another job anyway, in which case I'll still feel better. I'm going to do it," she said with a tone so determined that I was confident she meant it.

Several weeks later she returned to the office beaming. Her whole countenance was different now, for several reasons. One, the change in her diet had helped her not only to feel better, but to begin to lose unnecessary weight that she was carrying. She smiled more easily, her eyes were brighter. Today, I could tell there was something else that was different, too. "O.K., what is it?" I said with a grin, encouraging her to speak.

"I did it. I did it. Just like we discussed. The very next time my boss asked me if I would put in all those extra hours of overtime, I asked him how much he was going to pay me per hour? When he said, 'Nothing,' I said, 'No, you're asking me to do a lot, and I don't have any time to have a regular life. I've been doing this for a long time now, and it's starting to take its toll on my health. I just can't go on putting in all this overtime and not get paid for it. If you'd like to pay me time and a half, I'll be glad to put in extra hours.' "

We were both silent for a minute until I could stand it no longer, "Yes, and then what did he say?" I was eager to hear.

"He said, 'O.K.' "

"O.K., what?" I pressed.

"O.K., I didn't have to work overtime. They're on a fixed budget. I don't really think they can afford to pay me overtime. But he stopped asking me to work overtime and now I don't. Something else seems a little different, too," she continued. "I would have to say that it seems as if, well, maybe my boss respects me more. It seems as though he used to take advantage of me and now he doesn't."

"Does that surprise you?" I inquired. "After all, before you weren't acting like you respected yourself. You wouldn't speak up for yourself . . . wouldn't say no, when no was what you felt. Maybe now that *you* respect you, others are noticing it and sensing it as well."

"All I know is, it sure feels good," she smiled enthusiastically.

"Yes, I can tell that it does." Our smiles were genuine.

Lisa went on to make many other changes in her own life. I was simply there as a coach, making suggestions and recommendations about which changes might be helpful. She took the initiative and did them. The payoff from the changes belonged to both of us.

Using a combination of therapies, Cayce remedies, Chinese medicine, homeopathy, and clarification of mental and emotional ideals, Lisa was able to effect a great change in her life. There are still a few details to be corrected, to be sure, but isn't that true for most of us? Her tongue continues to be the "last frontier," a place where she still has periodic symptoms of discomfort. As for her other symptoms, she has recovered. Actually, she has done far more than simply recover. She has gone on to help, teach, and inspire others on their healing paths as well. Not a week goes by that she and I are not in contact.

After her great improvement began, people at work started asking questions—things like, "What are you doing? You're looking so good." Some of the other women wanted to know what she had said to the boss to gain her new-found respect. Lisa was not hesitant to tell them. "I simply learned to speak up for myself," she counseled confidently, "and you can do that, too." Her new-found confidence at work did not get her fired; it got her promoted. Instead of finding a new job, she simply found a new way to make the old job better.

Lisa has been instrumental in inviting a number of friends to healing workshops, like the "Change Your Mind, Change Your Life" workshops that I've presented. She knows that there are mental and emotional healing techniques that are a necessary part of the physical healing process, and she helps others find that out. I've seen others come to grips with their own problems because they were introduced to solutions by Lisa.

Lisa has also gone on to be a dedicated advisor and board member of the ECAFH Foundation (see the epilogue). Through her tireless efforts, she is working to bring the inspiration of complementary medicine to the general public. Her own dramatic healing has given her new sentiments and new perspectives on the art of medicine. Now recognizing the value of using many available forms of treatment, Lisa shares and spreads that news to others. When I made the announcement in Arizona that I would be moving to the state of Virginia, Lisa seemed genuinely sorry to know that I was going. The plaque she gave me, beautifully engraved inside a frame in the shape of the state of Arizona, is proudly displayed in my office. It is a tribute, I think, far more to her than to me. For it was through her own efforts that she has remade herself into a human dynamo. I'm proud that I was able to participate.

I display my plaque conspicuously. It reads:

Dr. Dana Myatt,

In appreciation for the excellent health care you have given me along with the many tools for promoting better health. Thanks for putting me on a path to the top.

Love and Hugs, Lisa B.

EPILOGUE

Janice came into my office nearly four months after I had first seen her. She was lean and muscular and walked with an easy gait. I wouldn't have recognized her except that I heard her announce her name to the receptionist.

"Janice, is it really you?" I was incredulous.

"Yes, it is, Dr. Myatt. I wanted to come and report back to you. I feel much better now."

Four months earlier, Janice had come into my office, moderately overweight and struggling with a cane. At that time, she told me she had been diagnosed with breast cancer some seven years before and had refused all forms of conventional treatment. No surgery, no chemotherapy, no radiation—and she was alive seven years after her diagnosis. Though she told me she had felt fine for most of those seven years, she recently had begun to have difficulties. "I'm not sure," she told me, "but I think the cancer might be in my bones. I don't want to go to 'regular' doctors. I'm afraid they will make me do some kind of treatment that I don't want."

"No one can make you do anything you don't want," I had advised her. "Though sometimes doctors seem to use intimidation techniques, the choice is still up to you. Tell me, why have you declined all conventional treatment?"

"Well," she explained, "I did a lot of research after my diagnosis. For the type of cancer I have, it really didn't look like the treatments were going to buy me much time, if any. On the other hand, the treatments had a lot of side effects that I just didn't want to endure. I believe that the body can heal itself. My best friend died from cancer even though she had treatment. I watched her become very sick from the chemotherapy. She was miserable all during the treatments, and she died in spite of them.

"I might die from the cancer," Janice told me, "but I don't want to be sick from the treatment. Especially if it doesn't look like it will help much. I just haven't been inspired to have any of the conventional therapies. Now I'm having some trouble, and I do think I need a little help. But I still don't want to take chemo or radiation. I plan on going to Mexico to a special clinic for some fasting and other treatments. What do you think?" she wanted to know.

"Well," I confirmed for her, "I certainly can't discourage you from that decision. You're right. What we have available from conventional medicine in your circumstance is really nothing. There are lots of different treatments for cancer, many of which are not allowed in this country. Nobody's got the market cornered on this disease—it's challenging in anybody's book. Still, people have gotten better from almost every method imaginable. I'd say, go for it. But why did you come to see me?"

"Well," she said, "I would like to have some of the conventional studies done. I need a doctor in this country to order the tests, but I won't go see an oncologist or an internist. I've done that before, and they always try to make me feel like I'm a bad person for not having the conventional treatments. Will you order the tests?" her voice had been pleading.

"Certainly. I'll be interested to see your 'before' and 'after' results . . . to see what improvements you make while on your special regimen in Mexico."

We ordered a bone scan and some blood and urine tests. They revealed that the cancer had spread and was affecting many areas of bone. From a conventional Western medical perspective, her circumstance was dire. She thanked me for ordering the tests and left.

Now she was back, the cane was gone, and she looked ever so much better. "I thought you'd like to see me and perhaps rerun some of those tests."

"Oh, yes, I certainly will want to do that. You look wonderful," I told her.

She described the treatments she had received in Mexico. They included a particular type of highly alkaline diet, digestive enzymes, and correction of a thyroid difficulty. Nothing amazing, really, and nothing that could not have been administered in this country. Yet she had been forced to travel far and wide to receive this kind of treatment. The reason? Because surgery, radiation, and chemotherapy drugs are the only accepted treatments for cancer in the United States.

Her repeat bone scans confirmed her improvement. The active areas of cancer in her bone had receded and were not as noticeable on the scan. Many of the different markers in the blood had also improved. Most important, the patient *felt* much better. No longer was she plagued by the pain in her bones. It was a case of a remarkable regression of a highly advanced cancer. Now the patient was back, curious and a little angry.

"Dr. Myatt, what I want to know is why did I have to go all the way to Mexico for these treatments? I should have been able to have them here. It was hard on me to be away from my friends and family for those months. Why don't big cancer centers in the United States tell people about the other things that can be done besides surgery, radiation, and chemotherapy?" Her voice was demanding. I had no certain answer, but I did have speculation.

I had a flashback to a day in medical school.

"One day," I told her, "I was in a manipulation class. Dr. Jack was my teacher. A student came in, raised her hand, and asked to tell about the weekend workshop she had attended. 'Dr. Jack,' she said, in a scolding tone, 'how come we're not learning the Rudolph technique in this class? It was a very good workshop, and I think it should be a part of our curriculum.'

" 'Well, it's like this,' Dr. Jack said in his characteristic slow drawl. He picked up a piece of chalk from the blackboard ledge and drew a huge circle on the board. 'This,' he said, pointing to the empty circle, 'is everything there is to know about healing. And this,' he said as he turned to the circle and drew a very tiny circle inside, 'is what you're learning in these next four years of medical school.' The room fell silent. 'And over here,' he said as he drew another tiny circle inside the large one, 'is what you would learn if you went to four years of allopathic medical school. And over here,' his drawl continued as he drew another small circle, 'is what you'd learn if you went to osteopathic medical school.' A voice in the back of the room chuckled.

" 'Now,' he said as he drew an even tinier dot inside the large one, 'this is what you learned last weekend at your workshop.' The student who had questioned him blushed.

" 'You gained a lot of good information. I encourage you all to take as many workshops and seminars as you can. You'll never learn it all.'

" 'And here,' he said, drawing yet another tiny circle, 'is everything you're going to be learning in this class.'

"He stopped talking and the room remained silent. The gist of his words was apparent. The human body is incredibly complex, the huge circle implied. No one in his or her entire lifetime will ever know all there is to know. No one from any particular school of medicine has all the answers either. His drawing made us humble.

"We understood," I concluded the story.

Then, I turned to the matter at hand. "Janice, that's a tough question to answer. Not because the answer is difficult to find, but because it's hard for me to say."

"Well, I know what you mean," she said. "Anything you say is your opinion. I'd like to know your opinion."

This woman had stared death in the eyes, made some difficult choices, and emerged, at least for now, victorious. How could I deny her this simple request?

"Well, I don't have to tell you that nobody seems to have the market cornered on healing. If any one school of healing knew everything, that would be the only school of thought we'd use. Success is popular. Since there are so many diseases that are 'incurable,' it's obvious to us all that nobody has all the answers.

"Politically speaking, however, there is one school of thought that has risen to power. It's not necessarily that any one school has answers that are more correct or more legitimate. It may not even be fair—in terms of freedom, I mean—to limit what our choices are. Right now, that's how we do things in this country. We only allow you access to one school of thought, one type of medicine. Oh, in truth, there are more things available. But you, more than most people, know how hard you have to work to get them. In many states, practitioners of complementary healing arts are denied the privilege of practice. And patients who seek this type of care are denied access to it and have to travel to faraway countries, like you did, to receive the treatment they choose."

"I wish," she said slowly, "that we could tell people that there are lots of different ways to heal."

"How can we educate people, help them know about their choices and help them make the *best* choices?"

"Well," I told her, "I've been thinking about this for many years myself. Now here you come along, begging the question to be answered. I've been meaning to find or create such an organization to do this education."

"Well," she said, "when do you plan to begin it?"

"Soon, maybe," was my hesitant answer. I had been "thinking about it" for many years. I also knew that simply thinking about an idea does not get the task accomplished. "I'll give this more serious thought," I told her sincerely and she seemed satisfied.

That night her question troubled me. I had indeed been intending for many years to find an organization (surely one existed) that was involved in educating the public about the many different directions from which healing can come. There must be an organization, if only I could find it, that kept track of all other health organizations. That way, when people called in, they could be advised of their choices or at least find out where to look. Instead of having to discover treatment options on their own from a sick bed, someone would be there to guide them, to help them know what was available. That organization would certainly make genuine statistics known—not just fallacy or superstition. I was sure that such an organization already existed, if only I could find it. And so, I *determined* to find it. Other patients would follow, I knew, like Janice. They would want to know everything that was available. They would *demand* it. With increasing awareness on the part of the public, more "Janices" would come. The next day I started my search in earnest.

There are many foundations, I discovered, that do research and collect information about specific illnesses. There are some foundations that are involved in educating the public about the full range of our health choices. There are even organizations that "watch dog" and try to prevent any one group from being the only health care options we have, simply on the basis of political power. I could not find one organization that was available for all these tasks. I mentioned this dilemma to Maxine, my former patient now volunteering as my executive secretary. "I'll look into it," she assured me and began to do research on her own. Her report to me confirmed my own studies. "There are lots of separate groups, each working on a part of this entire scene. I can't find one group that keeps track of all the other groups and makes all that information available to the general public. Maybe we should be involved in education and research on our own," she said.

Somehow I knew that was true, yet I resisted. "That would be a mighty big task," I reminded her.

"Well, yes and no," she said. "It would only succeed if those people who felt the same way were involved. I think there are enough interested folks to start a foundation."

Her words struck a familiar chord—one that I had heard being played inside myself for many years, but had always denied. Now the chord was played again, and I could ignore it no longer.

Exploring Complementary Answers For Health—ECAFH— was the name that came to us, mutually. Other people, many of them patients who have been healed, elected to become initial members of the foundation.

Our motto is "one mountain, many paths." The mountain is the high peak of health and wellness. The paths—you name it. Synthetic drugs, herbs, surgery, acupuncture, spinal manipulation—the list is long. Healing can come from many directions—always has, always will. We, more than any other country in the world—because we proclaim to be a country based on freedom—should have access to all the available choices. People need to have a resource of information, to find out what is known and is not known, what is true and what is false (again, so far as we know it). Making information readily available is the goal of the ECAFH Foundation.

Sometimes we call non-Western medicine "alternative." Most times, in fact. The National Institutes of Health has earmarked money (not much, but it's a start) to research some of these "alternatives." The problem is severalfold:

One, we want to "prove" alternative therapy by conventional standards. This denies the fact that there may be subtleties of the human body that cannot yet be placebo-controlled, double-blind studied.

Another problem is with our use of words. The term "alternative" implies "this *or* that." Either do it *my* way or do it *their* way. Nobody has all the answers. The most brilliant doctor in the world has only a few more answers than someone else. But put *all* the brilliant healers in the world together, combining their knowledge, and you have a few *more* pieces of the puzzle. What would happen if we combined the best of our knowledge and talent in a *complementary* fashion? Instead of this *or* that, what if our practice of medicine became this *and* that? The best of what is known from any direction that it comes?

My thoughts returned to Sadie, a patient of mine who lay in the cardiac intensive care unit, attached to numerous wires and monitors; her life was hanging by a fragile thread. Her carotid artery had ruptured and could do so again at any moment. Life was tenuous as she faded in and out of consciousness. As we stood by her bedside, we heard the alarm bell from other heart monitors. Because one nurse was watching twelve monitors, it was difficult to tell which one was Sadie's. Each time an alarm went off, I felt my heart race as I glanced at Sadie's EKG monitor. The alarm bell was never hers, but the fright was significant to me. "How much more was it affecting the patient?" I wondered as alarms went off. "What would happen if we took the best of what we knew from technology and combined it with the best of what we know from other disciplines?" I wondered to myself then as I do today.

Envision the same patient still attached to the high-tech heart monitor that informs the nurse or doctor of her status. Now envision soothing sounds and no alarms. A gentle form of music, perhaps baroque, at sixty cycles per second, the same rhythm we hope her heart will beat. What if the colors, the softly lit lights were selected on the basis of their ability to soothe and calm the patient? The nurse could read just as easily by a soft green light as she could by a dim, but irritating, small fluorescent light. And what if, during the course of her recovery, we fed her only the most excellent of healing foods and offered her herbs to stimulate her immune system? "Complementary" and "alternative" don't have to mean "low tech." When low tech is best, we use that. When high tech is best, we use that. When a combination of "techs" is best, whatever best serves the patient—that is what we use. Our goal is to use whatever "techs" are going to be most effective. The best answer probably lies some place in the middle. On that basis, our foundation continues to be Exploring Complementary Answers For Health.

For me personally, my work will always be heavily laced with the teachings and philosophy from the Edgar Cayce readings. But then, Cayce was a complementary psychic. His readings recommended treatments from all disciplines of the healing arts: conventional, unconventional—naturopathic, allopathic, osteopathic—every school of medicine was at one time or another recommended in the readings. I believe this was because Cayce's readings came from some "other dimension." Another dimension that we all, if we only knew how, would have access to. Cayce, perhaps because of his deep spirituality, was able to access this level of understanding. And at that deeper, purer level of understanding, his truth was this: no one has all the answers; we each have only a piece of the puzzle. That was clear from the readings when it came to issues of health. It was clear from the readings when it came to issues of religion or philosophy.

The work of the ECAFH Foundation is not "built" on the Cayce readings. Rather, it is in *agreement* with the readings. No one has all the answers; we each have a part. There is one mountain of truth to climb, but many paths lead to the mountaintop. Whether it be health, a study of the Supreme Being, or any other virtuous issue, there is more than one school of thought.

When we look carefully, we see that each of us holds but a single piece of a mighty puzzle. Our willingness to share information, exchange ideas, and cooperate rather than compete could greatly advance our understanding of life's mysteries, including the mystery of health and how to obtain it. Some of us will not be content as long as humankind is plagued by "dis-ease"—whether of body, mind, or soul. We will continue to look for truth wherever it exists. We will continue to explore contemporary answers for health. Will you?

THE END
(But it's really a new beginning . . .)

GLOSSARY

ALLOPATHIC—A system of medicine which uses substances to counter the symptoms of disease; in principle, the opposite of homeopathy. The term is often used to mean modern conventional medicine.

ENDOMETRIOSIS—A condition in which the membrane lining the inner surface of the uterus (the endometrium) is also found outside the uterus. This tissue responds to monthly female hormone changes and can result in bleeding in abnormal locations.

HOLISTIC MEDICINE—A philosophy of healing that considers a patient as a whole person rather than a disease or collection of symptoms. Many holistic practitioners combine conventional treatment with complementary treatment.

HOMEOPATHIC—A system of medicine that uses infinitesimal doses of natural substances, called remedies, to stimulate a person toward self-healing.

NATUROPATHIC—A system of medicine founded on the premise that the body is a self-repairing organism when given proper conditions. Naturopathic physicians are family practitioners trained in conventional and complementary medicine. They use nutrition, herbs, homeopathy, manipulation, counseling, and a variety of other natural therapies to assist the body in restoring itself to health.

OSTEOPATHIC—A system of medicine founded on the premise that the body can heal itself, especially if given the proper adjustment of bones, muscles, and nerves. Over time, the profession has so modified its original principles that it currently has moved closer to becoming similar to conventional (allopathic) medicine.

PERITONITIS—An inflammation of the peritoneum, a membrane that lines the abdominal cavity and viscera. The condition is extremely painful and often life-threatening.

RESOURCES

American Association of Naturopathic Physicians (AANP)
2366 Eastlake Avenue East, Suite 322
Seattle, WA 98102

Association for Research and Enlightenment, Inc. (A.R.E.)
Edgar Cayce Foundation
P. O. Box 595
Virginia Beach, VA 23451-0595

Atlantic University
P.O. Box 595
67th Street and Atlantic Avenue
Virginia Beach, VA 23451-0595

ECAFH Foundation, Inc.
10438 Oak Drive
Grass Valley, CA 95949

Naturopathic Colleges:
Bastyr College
144 NE 54th Street
Seattle, WA 98105

National College of Naturopathic Medicine
11231 S.E. Market Street
Portland, OR 97216

ABOUT THE AUTHOR

Dana Myatt, N.D., is a practicing family physician, teacher, public speaker, and writer.

Her study of the Edgar Cayce readings began at age twelve, and the readings were largely responsible for her decision to study *natural* healing methods. She graduated from the National College of Naturopathic Medicine in Portland, Oregon, in 1989, and served as both staff physician and director of medical residencies at the A.R.E. Clinic in Phoenix, Arizona. After working in family practice at the Scottsdale Holistic Medical Group, she relocated to Virginia Beach, where she taught anatomy/physiology at the Reilly School of Massotherapy and holistic health at Atlantic University. She continues her ongoing work as a family practitioner, workshop leader, and wellness educator.

What Is A.R.E.?

The Association for Research and Enlightenment, Inc. (A.R.E.®), is the international headquarters for the work of Edgar Cayce (1877-1945), who is considered the best-documented psychic of the twentieth century. Founded in 1931, the A.R.E. consists of a community of people from all walks of life and spiritual traditions, who have found meaningful and life-transformative insights from the readings of Edgar Cayce.

Although A.R.E. headquarters is located in Virginia Beach, Virginia—where visitors are always welcome—the A.R.E. community is a global network of individuals who offer conferences, educational activities, and fellowship around the world. People of every age are invited to participate in programs that focus on such topics as holistic health, dreams, reincarnation, ESP, the power of the mind, meditation, and personal spirituality.

In addition to study groups and various activities, the A.R.E. offers membership benefits and services, a bimonthly magazine, a newsletter, extracts from the Cayce readings, conferences, international tours, a massage school curriculum, an impressive volunteer network, a retreat-type camp for children and adults, and A.R.E. contacts around the world. A.R.E. also maintains an affiliation with Atlantic University, which offers a master's degree program in Transpersonal Studies.

For additional information about A.R.E. activities hosted near you, please contact:

A.R.E.
67th St. and Atlantic Ave.
P.O. Box 595
Virginia Beach, VA 23451-0595
(804) 428-3588